Pesach for the Rest of Us

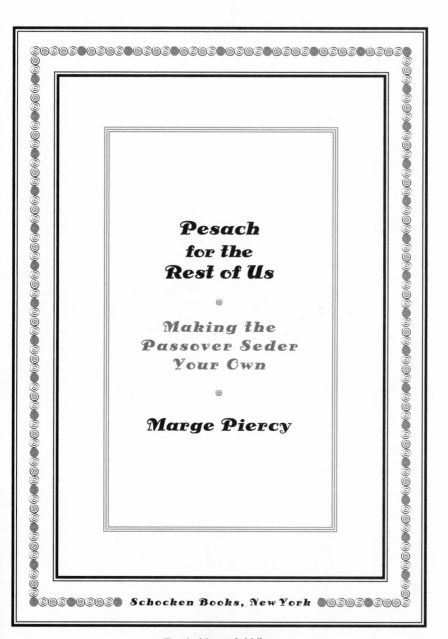

Pesach
for the
Rest of Us

⊚

Making the
Passover Seder
Your Own

⊚

Marge Piercy

Schocken Books, New York

296.45371
Pie

www.schocken.com

Book design by Iris Weinstein

Printed in the United States of America

First Edition

9 8 7 6 5 4 3 2 1

Feb 2007

Library of Congress Cataloging-in-
Publication Data

Piercy, Marge.

Pesach for the rest of us : making the
Passover seder your own / Marge Piercy.
p.   cm.

Includes bibliographical references
and indexes.

ISBN-13: 978-0-8052-4242-3
ISBN-10:   0-8052-4242-2

1. Passover—Customs and practices.
2. Seder.
3. Passover cookery.
4. Passover—Poetry.
I. Title.

BM695.P35P54 2007
296.4'5371—dc22   2006044381

For my Grandmother Hannah Levi Bunnin:
you did everything the right way
but loved us whatever we did,
in your memory

Contents

Pesach for the Rest of Us

1
What Kind of Book Is This and Who Is It For?

Pesach is a very important holiday for me. Every year, I lead a seder with a haggadah I have been working on for twenty years. Mostly the same people come from Boston, from New Jersey, from Arlington, Massachusetts, from two miles away, and from a quarter of a mile—we all gather gradually in my small Cape Cod house. Over the years, a couple and their children moved to Chile; some people tried it and it was not their kind of seder. One young woman grew up and now brings her husband. Children have been born and joined the seder. But basically we're pretty much the same core group year after year.

Like many Jews, Pesach is my favorite holiday and the one where I find the strongest personal meaning. I came to studying it earlier than Rosh Hashanah and Yom Kippur, perhaps because it is preeminently a holiday to share with family and friends. In this little book, I will make my way through the ritual one item and one practice at a time. I am looking for a significant contemporary interpretation, rather than an emphasis on what is strictly "correct" or traditional. I want to encourage you to fashion your own seder in a way that speaks honestly and powerfully to you and your circle, whoever they are—family, friends, an organization.

I often provide a historical perspective to help you choose or create a ritual that works for you. Much of what we may have been brought up with in modern Judaism in siddurs, in customary rituals of brit or bar or bat mitzvah, in holiday services or activities, was invented, worked out, haggled over, revised over many generations. You can borrow or create or combine to make a seder that works for your own group—whether family or friends or community. Try out new things every year. Keep the parts most people love or respond to and remember. Work on the parts that seem to put people to sleep.

The book is not aimed at the Orthodox, but rather at providing an entrance for secular and religious Jews with a modern slant into a more satisfying and meaningful way to celebrate our most common celebration, the one that just about every Jew partakes in, often twice with first and second night seders. Increasingly in recent years, Jews are putting together our own haggadahs or searching out material from other haggadahs to incorporate into our own ritual. There are literally thousands of haggadahs.

Many of us remember seders of our childhood where the haggadah was read mostly or entirely in Hebrew as fast as possible, usually by the patriarch of the family or some older man assuming that role. It had the emotional content of the directions for installing a DVD recorder. For many of us, that something has "always" been done a certain way does not mean that is how we want to do it or the way with the most meaningful content or spiritual resonance. Furthermore, Judaism is always changing. The way we celebrate Shabbat, the various parts of the services for Friday night and Saturday morning, the expectations concerning the holiday services, every piece of what "always" has been or what is "supposed to be" was started sometime in our history and kept because it worked for people. Other usages were gradually altered or dropped. The traditional haggadah has been evolving over centuries and adding some passages while dismissing others.

A commonly repeated statistic is that 90 percent of American Jews—no matter whether they are bagels and lox Jews or religious in some fashion or just in search of some sort of spirituality—attend at least one seder every Passover. That seder may be the only Jewish ritual a person engages in all year long and therefore the one experience that can confirm and give meaning to that person's Jewish identity. I am attempting to make elements of the haggadah and the seder rich with contemporary meaning so that the bored or deracinated adult would have an answer to, *Why do we go to all this bother every year?* or, *Why do I feel bereft if I have no seder to attend?*

Some people come to the seder wanting a spiritual experience. They want, not rote prayers or muttered blessings, but words and practices that move them, that awaken something in them that connects them to a sense of holiness and community. Some people come to the seder wanting to reconnect with a sense of the history of our people and to find something pertinent and engrossing in our identity as Jews. Some people come to the seder wanting to link up with the tradition of liberation in Judaism. Some people come just to eat, and that's okay too, as there is plenty of food for the stomach as well as the spirit. At Pesach we rededicate ourselves to what we cherish and what we find meaningful in our Jewish identity. We see ourselves as part of a people, historically and in the present. It is a time to remember that we as a people were once slaves and that people are enslaved in all eras and in many different ways. Slavery, whether literal or metaphorical, is very much with us today.

Thus inevitably Pesach has a political underpinning as we deal with issues of oppression and freedom, of revolt, of daring to change. For some, it is a time to rededicate ourselves to *tikkun olam*, the repair of the damaged world. A time to remember our thirst for justice and equality and to be inspired to resume the great work that will never be finished. Because like all Jewish holidays, Pesach has a seasonal reference, seders can also touch on ecological destruction and rebuilding. There can be an environmental aspect to the seder. All the way back to the days of the Talmud, Jews have argued about which aspect of the seder is the most important, the theme of liberation out in the world, resisting oppression, becoming free and helping others in their struggles for freedom, or internal liberation, fighting the inner as well as the outer Egypt. Really, we need not choose, for one without the other is weakened.

I believe that what all of these various desires have in common is a desire for connection: to what is eternal or to our history or to our people or to those, animal and vegetable, with whom we share this earth, or to those who are suffering or to those who seek to make the world fairer and gentler and better. A seder can give a sense of connection—spiritual or activist or communal or simply sensual. The traditional haggadah tells us that each Jew should feel as if she or he (it of course said *he*) personally was freed by the Exodus and left Egypt that night—an empathy across history that every haggadah tries to make happen in each individual who attends. Martin Buber urged us to feel a connection through history back to that first generation that dared seek freedom.

Thus a successful seder can try to satisfy many yearnings in the participants, different perhaps for each. But as Judaism is a religion of a people, not of an individual, the seder is a communal experience. We make it together. We make it for and with one another. Our alienation can be healed at least during that evening. We can experience a true sense of community at the seder table, one not based on something ephemeral or manufactured, like the crowd cheering at a football game, but a feeling of commonality that arises from real values.

The seder is a night to examine self and community, to choose to undergo the experience, to choose to join again as a Jew with other Jews, to question the tradition and the rituals, to wrestle meaning from them for each of us and the others with whom we are sharing the evening. *Erev Pesach* is a night for each of us to question what it means to be a Jew and what we want it to mean. How are we to be free? How are we to free ourselves and others? There are far more than four questions involved in a true Pesach experience.

We also crave redemption. We see ourselves as flawed and the world as broken, aching, bleeding. This is a time when we call ourselves to account, not in the sense of the Days of Awe, but in a more social sense. What are we doing to fight oppression? What are we doing to make things better? There is no agenda. Each person should find the work of redemption that touches their innermost values and sense of how things ought to be as opposed to how they are. That is part of the story of the Exodus, the rising in revolt against what is unfair and painful and unjust. We remember our history on Pesach, but we also look at our present and contemplate the future we might want to make happen and the future we passionately want to avoid—for ourselves, our children, our grandchildren, for all those beings with whom we share this earth.

My grandmother Hannah created the seders of my childhood. My grandfather Morris was killed before I was born, so I never met him directly—only through family stories. Among my early good memories are seders in her apartment in Cleveland, with several of my mother's brothers and sisters gathered around a long table. Somebody was always missing, particularly during World War II, when two of my uncles were already dead, one of a plane crash (he was a stunt pilot in air shows) and one of pneumonia, and one was in the Merchant Marine, at sea. My two oldest aunts lived out in Everett, Washington, and during the war, Aunt Rose was still dancing, entertaining the troops, but there were plenty of us. My grandmother had borne nine children who lived into adulthood, five men and four women including my mother. They all had husbands or wives and some had children at the seder.

Grandmother Hannah was poor and Orthodox, like her father the rabbi, and she kept the laws strictly. She might not own a coat that wasn't repaired and she might not have daily clothes that were not frayed and worn, but she had dishes only for Passover and a spotless tablecloth saved for good occasions. She had fine silver candlesticks brought from Lithuania where she had grown up in the shtetl. I don't know what happened to them. Like so much else in my tumultuous family, they disappeared.

She lived with us for part of every year, sharing my bed, and I remember her lush long brown hair thatched with silver worn around her head in braids and then at night let loose so it cascaded down her back. I remember her brown eyes dimmed with cataracts, her back stooped with labor, her slightly husky voice telling stories from the shtetl and from women's rich lore. She did not wear a wig because my grandfather had forbidden it, and after his death she kept faith with him.

In my childhood, she did not serve lamb for Passover but beef. It is a family tradition I maintain and my seder guests would be peeved if I made anything else. (Vegetarians, do not worry! There are many vegetarian recipes throughout.)

◎

Gedempte Flaisch mit Abricotten

You need a piece of flanken or a chuck roast. The size depends on the number of people you are serving. I usually allow about ⅓ pound per person, but if I were serving it on another occasion when there is less to eat before it is served, then I would allow more.

I marinate the pot roast in red wine or Madeira with onions, garlic, some allspice, salt, a little olive oil, and herbs as you like. I use a standard bouquet garni. I let it stand in the marinade overnight or for a few hours, depending on my schedule.

I soak dried apricots in sweet kosher wine for an hour, separate from the meat. I like the whole organic pitted Turkish apricots.

Preheat the oven to 350°F.

I pause here and cut up carrots, a couple of parsnips, more onions, and more garlic. The amount of vegetables increases with the weight of your meat. Do not skimp. They will be delicious.

I drain the meat and carefully dry it, keeping the marinade. I brown it until seared on all sides. Then I take it out, turn down the heat, and gently cook the onions for 5 minutes, then add the garlic, the carrots, and the parsnips.

If you like, you can add ginger or cinnamon.

After another 5 or 6 minutes, I put the meat back in with the marinade and add more wine if necessary (it usually is). I also add the apricots with the wine they are soaking in. Bring it to a boil on the stove, then immediately put it in the oven. It cooks until completely tender and you should turn it a couple of times. For a 6-pound roast, I roast it 2½ hours if using chuck; 3 hours if using flanken. I want it done just before the seder starts. Remember to turn off the oven! One year I didn't and the pot roast resembled charred wood. It will sit happily in the oven until you reach the point in the seder when it is time to eat.

◎

For some Jews lamb is traditional because of its association with Pesach; for others, it is avoided because of the destruction of the Temple. I love lamb, and if I wasn't honoring the memory of my bubelah, I would probably serve lamb.

◎

Cinnamon Lamb

Leg of lamb
3 eggs
3 tablespoons potato flour or fine matzoh meal
Black pepper to taste
1 teaspoon cinnamon
½ teaspoon cloves
½ teaspoon salt
Finely chopped parsley or basil or mint or a combination
Juice of 2 lemons

Score the lamb. Beat the eggs and then mix all the other ingredients. Fill the cracks and cover the outside of the lamb with the paste made from above items. Let it sit half an hour. Roast normally.

This lamb has a nice crust with flavor that penetrates the meat while it is cooking. How many it feeds depends on the size of the leg and how much else you are serving.

◎

Food is a strong carrier of tradition. Families have dishes they hand down. Part of what I cook on the various holidays is what my grandmother cooked before me, learning from her mother. When I eat certain dishes, I am partaking of the lore of my ancestors. When I cook Sephardic or Mizraki, I am sharing in a tradition perhaps older than my family's Ashkenazi cooking, and I feel joined to those communities of Jews as well as that of my more immediate ancestors. Food sometimes feels like emotion made edible. It is one more way of feeling connected.

My grandmother, who thought herself uneducated because she knew only scanty Hebrew, presided in a moral sense, cooking the meal, fussing, making everything as nice and pretty as she could, but she deferred to whichever son was present to lead the seder. It was all in Hebrew so I never understood it until I was much older. My brother was taught Hebrew for his bar mitzvah, but, being a girl, I was not given one and learned no Hebrew until I was saying kaddish for my mother. I began to study Hebrew then and was finally bat mitzvahed at age fifty.

My grandmother's gentleman cat, Blackie, always attended the seder, having a chair of his own. He did not, however, read the haggadah. I was not convinced that he could not talk, but I understood that he, like me, had not been taught Hebrew.

Learning to read

My mother would not teach me to read.
Experts in newspapers and pop books
said school must receive us virgin.
Secrets were locked in those

black scribbles on white, magic
to open the sky and the earth.
In a book I tried to guess from
pictures, a mountain had in its side

a door through which children ran in
after a guy playing a flute
dressed all in green, and I too
wanted to march into a mountain.

When I sat at Grandmother's seder,
the book went around and everybody
read. I did not make a distinction
between languages. Half the words

in English were strange to me.
I knew when I had learned to read
all would be clear, I would know
everything that adults knew, and more.

Every handle would turn for me.
At school I grabbed words like toys
I had been denied. Finally I
could read, me. I read every sign

from the car. On journeys I read
maps. I read every cereal box
and can, spelling out the hard words.
All printing was sacred.

At the seder I sat down at the table,
self-important, adult on my cushion.
I was no longer the youngest child
but the smartest. When the hagaddah

was to be passed across me,
I grabbed it, roaring confidence.
But the squiggles, the scratches
were back. Not a letter

waved to me. I was blinded again.
That night I learned about tongues.
Grandma explained she herself spoke
Yiddish, Russian, Polish, Lithuanian

and bad English, little Hebrew.
That's okay, I said. I will
learn all languages. But I was
fifty before I read Hebrew.

I no longer expect to master
every alphabet before death
snatches away everything I know.
But they are always beckoning to me

those languages still squiggles
and noises, like lovers I never
had time to enjoy, places
I have never (yet) arrived.

I remember the first year I was permitted to light the candles and say the blessings, and how jealous I was when my uncle Danny's daughter was the youngest at table and read the four questions instead of me. I loved the seders, even though I cannot pretend that as a child, I grasped the meaning. It was the ritual I found beautiful—the formality interspersed with joking and laughter, the shape of the evening, and, of course, being allowed to sip sweet wine four times. I don't remember much else that Hannah served except that she began with a hard-boiled egg and chicken soup. Dessert was macaroons and dates.

After my grandmother died, when I was fifteen, the family seders ended. My father wasn't about to let my mother put one on; he was not Jewish and not religious. In fact, he scorned any religious activities. Over the next few years, I attended seders with various friends—at their houses, one put on by Hillel at college, one with a group of graduate students in Chicago. I even tried to put one together myself with my first husband, but I did not have enough money to buy lamb or beef. Everyone had a little bit of chicken. We mumbled away at a haggadah somebody's family used, without much resonance. Still, it was better than nothing, which is what I had for years with my second husband. Although he was Jewish, he was in rebellion against all observation. It wasn't until I was living part-time in a commune in Cambridge that I began to take part in seders again. We used a Reform haggadah—probably the Maxwell Coffee one—and each contributed a dish. I was very happy to share Pesach with them. After I became involved with my present husband, we began to host our own.

I met Ira Wood on Pesach. I was in Cambridge, Massachusetts, staying at my commune. It was afternoon and I was walking down a street behind the Martin Luther King School, going to visit an old friend of mine who lived upstairs in a cheap rental in a decrepit two-story frame house. On the front porch, a young man was standing beating egg whites. My friend had told me that he had become close to the guy living downstairs. Indeed, this man from downstairs seemed to know who I was and introduced himself. He was beating the egg whites in a desultory manner—languid, you might say. We have wondered since what he could have been making. His memory is potato kugel, a strange dish for Pesach but his attempt to create something he remembered from his grandmother's table. In any event, I could see that he was never going to get the egg whites whipped the way he was going at it. So I took the bowl from him and beat them until they were stiff. In the meantime, we talked. I found him charming. When I went home, I told one of my female friends that I had met a cute and great guy, but he was probably gay. My stereotype. I didn't know any other men besides gay friends who cooked or would bring something fancy to a seder.

So I met the best husband I would or could have in the afternoon just before Erev Pesach. We got involved in June, married six years later in 1982, and have been together ever since. It was a couple of years after Ira and I began living full-time on Cape Cod that I started to hold the seders here. Over the twenty-odd years since, children have been born, grown up, married, and still come. Some of the couples are mixed, and this seder has been their children's introduction to Judaism. It has sparked an interest that several have pursued. For some of us, it is the only time of year we see each other, and yet over the years we have come to feel warmly about everyone. Every year, I add or change a little of my ongoing haggadah. The poems that are part of many chapters of this book are from my haggadah, with a couple of exceptions, like the poem about learning to read. Eventually I expect 90 percent of the haggadah to be poetry; now it is about 65 percent. We sit around the table in our small dining room, fifteen of us—

sometimes more—all the room will hold. We are crowded together and anyone getting out of his or her seat has to inconvenience several other people, but everyone seems jolly about the close quarters. After we have finished the haggadah, we sit around the table stuffed and happy, and tell jokes. Everyone tries to come up with new jokes for the seder, including the kids. Some of us are great natural comics, but some, like me, cannot remember a joke unless we write it down. I think I have mastered a total of six jokes in my lifetime, and that could be an overestimate. Finally we have coffee and people slowly drift out into the night. Some have a hundred miles to drive; some live nearby. The friend from New Jersey stays over.

Now, although my grandmother in some sense presided over the seders of my childhood, the haggadah was always read by one of her sons. Judaism was presented in my childhood as a male activity. Women had a lot of work to do, kitchen work, but men were the real Jews. Women have over the past century been demanding that Judaism speak to us, serve and acknowledge our experiences, our needs, our humanity. If women are truly Jews, then we need a practice that recognizes us—not one from which we are excluded, exiled. Not one in which our role is only to cook and serve and keep quiet. Not one in which we are included only as pseudo-men. We desire a practice that on every level, from its concerns to its language and structure, includes us.

You may notice that I avoid the masculine terms for what is eternal and I also try to avoid God language that seems to me to embody patriarchal patterns of thought or ways of viewing what's holy, that infantilize us or cast us into archaic forms of address— like Lord. Often I use Shekinah, the feminine aspect of The Eternal, to remind us that the holy is both masculine and feminine. I will include two items that women have added to the haggadah in the past twenty-five years, the orange on the seder plate and Miriam's cup, to complement Eliyahu's cup. This is not a book in which when I write "a Jew," you should see in your mind's eye a man or a boy. If when I write Hashem or The Eternal, you visualize an old man with a white beard, you are in the wrong book. I take the kabbalistic view that what is holy enters into the world in both masculine and feminine aspects, but that when you penetrate through your practice into what is eternal, it is neither male nor female.

The concept of God in the traditional haggadah works for very religious Jews but for many of us is off-putting or something we simply ignore. We may not believe in miracles or a Supreme Being who intervenes in history. We may not believe in a Supreme Being at all. We may believe there's something eternal but not a personal God. Whatever we believe, as Jews we need a practice that works for us on Pesach.

So welcome to a journey through the items on the seder plate, the other ritual items, the foods we consume, the parts of the haggadah, in an attempt to renew their significance for us, together, at our tables. My intent is to stimulate your practice and make it more resonant, more enjoyable, more engaging, more thoughtful and conscious. Whatever haggadah or haggadahs you use, I hope this book will complement it and enrich your experience of Pesach.

2
Chametz

There are many books that tell one how a Jew is supposed to prepare for Pesach. Many of these requirements are particularly onerous for women. Four sets of dishes—one for meat, one for dairy, meat dishes for Pesach, and dairy dishes for Pesach—may work for someone with a big house and lots of cupboard space. However, if you have only a tiny kitchen as I do, or you live in an apartment, there may be absolutely no way. Nor can I afford or store four sets of silverware or four sets of pots and pans. I barely have room for one set. With the amount of cooking I do, I would love a large kitchen with an attached pantry, but short of knocking down the cement block walls of the bottom story, chopping down some big beautiful trees I planted decades ago, and encroaching on the garden—and winning a lottery or robbing a bank to afford the renovation—it isn't going to happen. I have often observed, by the way, that the fanciest, best-equipped, and roomiest kitchens often seem to exist in the houses of those who do little or no cooking.

To do things properly according to kashrut requires that the whole house be kashered, especially the kitchen and any cooking, eating, or mixing utensils or surfaces. Kashering of kitchen utensils requires immersion in boiling water. Other cooking utensils are kashered in a superhot oven—set to broiling and kept there for an hour or more. Some use a blowtorch or pour boiling water over surfaces. Some women use a hot iron to kasher the drain boards and working surfaces. If you are interested in preparing a totally "correct" kosher household, there are many how-to books and books on Passover that include detailed instructions. It would be hypocritical for me to lay out those rules, as I do not observe them. I recommend Blu Greenberg's *How to Run a Traditional Jewish Household*.

Many of the food strictures require a woman who is home and has a great deal of time to give. Some contemporary women do all of this and enjoy it; keeping complete and proper kosher is relevant for them and worth the effort. I have friends who observe all the dietary laws and find pleasure and meaning in kitchen kashrut. The sense of tradition is comforting and gives a historical resonance to the work. They see themselves, as I do when I am lighting Shabbat candles, as one in a long line of women stretching back into our history and prehistory, all of them in some sense contained in me as I perform the ritual act. Some women have a strong sense of a personal deity whom they please by obeying. I understand this piety, but I also understand that for many Jewish women, the housework around Pesach is burdensome and gives them all the spiritual zing of doing the laundry on a heavy day three times over.

My own religious education from my grandmother Hannah was Orthodox, but I already knew when I was fifteen that following strict halachah (Jewish law) would not work for me. I feel strongly Jewish, but I also knew I wasn't going to go through all the women's work that my grandmother carried out to keep a kosher home. I remember her preparations for Pesach, but with a kind of horror for all it put her through. I would rather put that time into preparing the haggadah—I do some rewriting every year. I would rather meditate about the meaning of Pesach than iron the kitchen counters. Whenever I read one of the books that tell you how to prepare for Pesach, I notice the verbs: the oven *is turned to* broil for an hour; the kitchen counters *are scoured;* utensils used all year must *be heated* until they glow red. It reads as if these counters scrubbed themselves; or perhaps angels come down and do it. The women who actually carry out all this hard work are invisible. There can be holiness in cleaning, in women's work, which I don't mean to denigrate. It's just true that for many of us, there is no inner meaning. We clean when we absolutely have to, but we never have time to clean the way our mothers did in the Golden Age of Housework.

More relevant in discussing kashrut is the fact that 47 percent of the nation's Jews who married since 1996 chose non-Jews.* In my own family and my husband's, I have seen children of mixed marriages raised as Christians. Sometimes it seems easier to the Jewish spouse; sometimes conversion is the result of ignorance of their own traditions and a lack of any way to make them relevant. However, I have also seen in my seders and in the work of devoted women in our havurah how the children of mixed families can come to feel proudly Jewish. Just this month, as I am writing, I took part in a bar mitzvah for a boy of mixed parentage who sang his Torah portion perfectly and gave a moving speech about

*Michael McCarthy, "Have a Merry Little Chrismukkah," *USA Today,* December 16, 2004.

his portion—one of the most beautiful such occasions I've ever attended. The family, including the father, who was not Jewish, put an enormous amount of heart and mind into making a ceremony that combined tradition with contemporary Jewish sources.

It is not inevitable that the children of mixed marriages will forget their heritage and join the vast non-Jewish majority. But it requires a sense of how to take parts of tradition and ritual and make them meaningful. Judaism cannot be all or nothing, as many Orthodox believe, if there are to continue to be Jews. It is important in any family to create rituals that bring the members together and create a sense of the turning year and the history that led to our own lives. These experiences can be both personal and communal; the rituals can provide a sense of roots but also mean something in the present, so that the words are not gibberish, not boring recitation, but something that touches that child.

In Torah it says that there shall be no leaven in the house for all the days of Pesach. That means no bread—except matzoh made without yeast—no wheat, barley, rye, oats, or spelt. In my childhood, I invariably asked, "What is spelt?" My grandmother said she thought it was some kind of dried pea or bean. *The Cambridge World History of Food* defines it as a type of wheat similar to rye. Today you can find it in whole food stores.

Vinegar made from grain is also considered chametz. In Ashkenazi—Jews from Germany and Eastern Europe and their descendants—usage, chametz also means no rice, no dried legumes such as peas and lentils, no parched corn. In Sephardic—Jews expelled from Spain and Portugal who spread across the Mediterranean and to the Netherlands, and their descendants—and Mizraki—Jews from the Arab countries—usage, beans are not always forbidden and rice is often found in Pesach dishes. In

Ashkenazi usage, there is an avoidance of what's called *kitniyot*—little bits of things like sesame seeds or sunflower seeds and their by-products. The definition of chametz gets very elaborate. Basically, *kitniyot* are the small seeds of annual plants that might be ground into flour. Some people avoid ketchup, brown sugar, peanuts and peanut products, corn oil, mayonnaise, and soy products. Over the years in Ashkenazi usage, the forbidden list has grown and grown. If you feel good about excluding all kinds of things that have no precedent in Torah, you should do so. Some find comfort in carrying out strict and detailed edicts. But if this list seems arcane and arbitrary to you, forget it. Neither Sephardic nor Mizraki Jewry forbid all these foods. I sometimes imagine groups of rabbis in the Middle Ages gathering to play trivia games to see how many common foodstuffs could go on the no-no list.

In our havurah, we always had a second-night seder for the community, when up to 180 people would come. We'd ask people to bring one dish big enough for six people. The havurah would provide the paper plates, plastic utensils, gefilte fish, kosher wine, grape juice, and ritual items for every table. Sometimes a participant would become furious and berate some other cook for providing a dish that was acceptable for Pesach under Sephardic rules but not under Ashkenazi usage—usually something with rice. Every time it would be my duty to explain those different customs. Sometimes that would quiet everybody down, but I still remember the woman who stood there quivering with righteous anger, saying, "That may be *their* custom, but it's wrong!"

This reminds me of arguments that can break out about which melody is proper for singing "Adon Olam" or any other old song that has five or six or more melodies, each of which is traditional to the particular synagogue, nationality, or family habit of some person. Jews can be very parochial and extremely attached to a particular way of doing some religious act or reciting some prayer or singing some part of the service—and claim that their own way is the only right one.

Well before Passover, it is traditional to begin removing forbidden grains from the household. If you are a member of a synagogue or a well-organized havurah, you can probably collect the forbidden products in your home and "sell" them as your synagogue has arranged. Then you get them back after the seven or eight days of Passover. You have to go to the work of collecting, cleaning, and toting, but that's it.

Many Jews don't belong to a synagogue. Maybe they're in a casual havurah or maybe they have no organizational affiliation. If they can afford the time and money, then they can discard or burn their chametz. I never assume, as some people seem to, that all Jews have money. I grew up in a working-class household where there was plenty of nothing besides bills and trouble. If you are a single mother or single father with kids, or living alone, or working two or three jobs to survive, this waste is just beyond you. If you have a shed or a garage, you could store chametz there. You do want to remove it from where it could be accidentally used during Pesach.

The search for chametz and the removal of it can be a joint effort with partners or kids, or you can even turn it into a small party with friends. The search is called *bedikat chametz*. You do it room by room. Rooms that are never eaten in, not even snacks, you may skip, unless you are combining the search for chametz with a regular spring cleaning—if you do that. Look in seat cushions, under couches and chairs. Turn out pockets. Traditionally, *bedikat chametz* is done with a feather, a wooden spoon, and a candle in Ashkenazi usage; in Sephardic custom, a candle, a knife, and a wooden bowl are used. You can even hide tiny packets of bread around the house, organizing a search party. This is an old custom. I remember my grandmother hiding ten chunks of bread wrapped in a bit of paper in her apartment. You are supposed to go with a candle and a feather but my grandmother had been through two fires, so she used a flashlight. I never knew exactly what I was supposed to do with the feather; still, it was fun and I carried it around.

The next step is *vittul chametz*: if you missed anything, you ask that it be nullified. After that, technically it doesn't exist. Then comes the fun part: *bi'ur chametz*. Take your kids or your partner or your friends and symbolically burn some breakfast cereal and the chametz you collected. Even if you didn't bother scouring the house for chametz, the miniature bonfire can provide a sense of getting ready for the holiday. If you don't have a patio or yard to use, you can burn your crumbs in a hibachi or in a big pan on the stove, in a fireplace or woodstove, or in some receptacle in the bathtub (which is where I light my *yahrzeit* candles every year). You could trot off to a local playground or some other safe area, if it *is* safe where you live, and build your tiny bonfire there—but you don't want to get your kids or yourself into trouble. As a last resort, you could burn some chametz in an ashtray.

My own usage is sloppy and heavy on the convenient. During the weeks leading up to Passover, I try to cut down on purchases of chametz, so that there is less to deal with. The birds have a feast when I get rid of cookies, crackers, bread, and old cereal. But I have to drive thirty-four miles to purchase whole grain products such as kasha, cracked wheat (bulgur), and brown rice.

In the interest of ecology and economy, I simply put all those products that are not yet opened in my storeroom and leave them there for the duration of Passover. Some people put all the chametz into a cupboard and tape it shut. Some people store it in a garage or shed, but be warned: the mice may get into it. My cats patrol my storeroom; they like Pesach just fine.

Why get rid of chametz? So much fuss about something we eat every day. Well, originally it might have had something to do with the historical probability that leavened bread was invented in Egypt. Lighter, fluffier bread was the food of the higher echelons of the hierarchy—overseers, aristocrats, princes, scribes. The original daily bread was just a kind of gritty gruel baked on flat stones. That was one of the first prepared foods in the Middle East. So you are bidden to go back to origins.

Leaven can also metaphorically stand for pride, for what puffs us up, for a kind of luxury introduced but unnecessary. It can stand for what there is in us that keeps us from doing what we should, *yetzer ha-ra*, the inclination to do wrong or to refrain from doing right. We will delve further into the meaning of matzoh in chapter 11. Judaism is full of divisions: clean and unclean animals, dairy and meat, Jews and others. Sometimes our understanding of these divisions can divide us one from the other. At Pesach, bread, which at other times of year we bless and share every Shabbat, turns into an emblem of conceit, of all that inflates us and makes us feel superior.

Notions of what is appropriate and "clean" depend upon context. There is nothing dirty about clean underwear, but we would not want it used as napkins at dinner. Shoes are fine on our feet but not in bed. We grow our food in dirt but do not wish it on the table. Context defines what we consider appropriate, clean, correct. In the context of Pesach, bread represents what we want to get rid of.

To me, to observe the rituals in which I can find meaning and a strong identification as a Jew is far more important than to follow laws defined and redefined and haggled over for millennia. I respect those who follow every stricture recognized in their Jewish community, but I want to be inclusive, not hypercorrect. I want a myriad of Passovers, one for every household, every apartment, every Jew of whatever age and background and belief. For every one of us, I want a Pesach we can carry out with pleasure and fervor, one that gives us insight into our lives, one that strengthens us as Jews and as moral and committed human beings. For me, avoiding sunflower oil is pointless; concentrating on a long list of dubious value takes away from the resonance of Pesach.

In the recipes I include in various chapters, I have usually followed Ashkenazi usage as to chametz, but I include Sephardic dishes of which I am especially fond or which I think you may find delicious and attractive. I include some Sephardic dishes with rice, in case that is the custom you prefer. Sometimes I think that the farther our ancestors got from *Eretz Yisrael* (the Land of Israel), the stricter and more complicated became their usages and prohibitions.

It's not hard to do without bread for eight days—people following a low-carb diet do it all the time. It gives you a little challenge to cook without any of the grains you are used to, but it's not that difficult. I'll include a few recipes that work for Pesach, that you can cook for any meal in the week. There are many more in chapter 11 on matzoh and chapter 19, "The Feast."

◎

Pesach Tzimmes

Mince 4 carrots. A food processor does this very quickly. Don't continue until they are mush.

Chop a sizable white or yellow onion.

Begin sautéing them together in chicken fat (I actually use goose fat) or olive oil, unless you are making a dairy meal. Then butter or olive oil works just fine.

Core 2 or 3 tart, well-flavored apples. Don't bother to peel them. Chop them. Add them with some kosher wine. Not too much. Add a little salt, some ground coriander, and some ground ginger. Cook it on top of the stove in a covered pan, stirring occasionally and adding a bit more kosher wine if you like. If you can't stand kosher wine, use some dry Madeira or sherry. Keep the flame relatively low, but high enough to cook it.

If you like, after you have cooked the dish for an hour, add some farfel—small pieces of matzoh. Don't add too much. Go light on this.

Cook for another 30 minutes and taste it. I have seen tzimmes recipes that cook the dish for hours, but I find that an hour and a half works just fine for this.

It reheats well.

◎

Here's another hearty dish.

◎

Beef or Lamb Matzoh Pie

You want 4 cups of good beef broth. The Israeli cubes work fine. Boil the water, put in the cubes, mix well and let it cool.

4 cups almonds or walnuts
1 pound ground beef or ground lamb
1 big yellow onion minced
6 sheets matzot
½ cup of water or leftover dry red wine
Salt
Pepper
1 egg, beaten
Whatever herbs you fancy: Fresh parsley or basil, fresh
    rosemary chopped very fine, or, if you are using dried
    herbs, fines herbs

Preheat the oven to 325°F.

Chop almonds or walnuts in a food processor briefly. You don't want to create a paste. You want little pieces still identifiable as nuts.

Brown the meat, stirring wildly. Add onion. Then add the liquid, cover, and cook for about ten minutes.

Moisten the sheets of matzoh in the broth, just enough to soften it. Don't let it come apart. Put 4 sheets in two layers on the bottom of the greased casserole you're going to use. Add the meat filling and then use the remaining sheets to make a cover.

Moisten more matzoh if you need more. Glaze the top of the pie with the beaten egg. If you have a little brush, it's easier than using a knife. Add the chopped nuts spread evenly over the top. Gently pour the broth over all. Add the herbs.

Bake @ 325 for an hour. This and a salad could make a nice supper for family during Passover and uses some of that matzoh lying around getting stale after the seder. This would feed four or five.

◎

There are actually many dishes we make all the time that do not involve chametz and are convenient and pleasant during Pesach. Avoiding chametz is not the worst deprivation, for it reminds us that we are in a special season with special meanings. It keeps us alert to the thoughts and reactions and insights we may experience during the seder.

3
Candlelighting

Besides cooking the meal and setting the table, there is one more task to perform as evening approaches: setting up the seder plate. One traditional way to set up the seder plate goes back to the Maharal, Judah Loew. I have a particular fondness for him (he is one of the characters in my novel *He, She and It*) so I am partial to his ordering. He was the head rabbi in Prague in 1600, a kabbalist, a friend of Tycho Brahe and Johannes Kepler—and he is often associated with the Golem tale. He was one of those Renaissance men with one foot in the Middle Ages and one foot in modernity.

BEYTZAH   Z'ROAH

MAROR

KARPAS   CHAROSET

CHAZERET

That puts the three items required by Torah at the top and the three added later at the bottom. A common Sephardic arrangement follows. Sephardic plates are usually bigger than Ashkenazi seder plates and have room for the matzot. The matzot are at the top of the plate.

MATZOT

BEYTZAH   Z'ROAH

MAROR

KARPAS   CHAROSET

CHAZERET

We light candles to mark off the beginning of Shabbat from the rest of the week. At the end of Shabbat, we douse the braided havdalah candle in wine to mark the end of the holiday. We light candles at the opening of festivals—at Rosh Hashanah, for instance. We light them at the beginning of each seder. If a seder falls on Shabbat, we light two sets of candles. In Ashkenazi usage, often there are two candles, but in Sephardic custom, there are seven candles for Pesach.

Lighting the candles separates the day that is ending from the day that is beginning—at sunset—and separates the ordinary from the holy. It is an act of transformation. We are to focus ourselves and move into an alternate space, one of being open to the meaning of the ritual to follow. It also resonates with the beginning of the Torah: *And Hashem said, "Let there be light"; and there was light. Hashem saw that the light was good, and separated the light from the darkness. Hashem called the light Day, and the darkness, Night. And there was evening and there was morning, the first day.* So you are separating the holy from the ordinary. Light metaphorically represents en-light-enment—spiritual, inner light.

But before you light the candles, if you live someplace where what I am about to suggest is possible, then this may bring home to you and your guests that the Jewish calendar is a lunar calendar. Go outside and face the east. If it is a relatively clear night, the full moon of Nisan should be rising there. It is a way of beginning the seder with a reminder of what the calendar is based upon and giving a bit of a connection to nature. Most people at my seder come here from cities and I doubt if they notice the moon any other time. Here the moon rises across the marsh and hangs in the trees that are not yet leafed out or sometimes not even budded.

Now back in and to the candles. As you light them, you should say a blessing. Here is the traditional blessing in masculine Hebrew:

Baruch atah Adonai (if you are comfortable with Lord, continue; but if you find it archaic, you might want to replace it with *Hashem* or *Ein Sof*) *Eloheynu Melech Ha-Olam asher kideshanu b'mitzvotav v'tzivanu l'hadlik ner shel* (if it is Shabbat add here *Shabbat v'shel*) *Yom Tov.*

Here it is in the feminine:

Bruchah at Shekinah eloheynu ruach ha-olam asher kideshatnu b'mitzvoteha v'tzivatnu l'hadlik ner shel (Shabbat v'shel) yom tov.

Basically any blessing you want to say in English is just as good. Traditional blessings work when people are familiar with the Hebrew. Otherwise, they convey nothing. To bless, you must feel the blessing as an act. I was at one seder years ago where they sang "This little light of mine" and that seemed to work just as well. If you bless in your own words, sometimes you mean it much more.

I like to use Hannah Senesh's poem "Blessed is the match" with the lighting of the candles. Senesh gave up a life of safety in Israel to parachute into occupied Yugoslavia and was executed in her native Hungary by the Nazis. She gave her life in an attempt to help liberate her people. Remembering her seems appropriate at this time. You can find her poem, translated by Marie Syrkin, in Syrkin's volume *Blessed Is the Match* and in *Hannah Senesh: Her Life and Diary* (Jewish Lights, 2004).

If it is Shabbat, here is an alternate blessing, not a translation.

This is to be read responsively:

As the great doors of night are opening
we come into the clean quiet room of Shabbat.

Let us be thankful, as we light these candles
like eyes of holiness, for this moment of peace.

Let us savor the fruit of the vine,
grape that has changed into sweet fire.

Let us be thankful for grain, fruit of grasses
that feed the cow, the horse, and us.

Let us be grateful for children and the work
of the week that is our fruitfulness.

Let the doors of our minds open wide
as night and welcome in the peace of Shabbat.

Here as the first words of the ritual are spoken, you want something to focus you. People come in from all the places they have journeyed from. People who have attended before, some since birth, greet each other; many have not met since the last seder. There is casual socializing and reacquainting. Allow time for interaction before you sit people down and begin. I ask people to come a good half hour before we start. You want people's full attention, as much of it as you can grab when you actually begin the ritual. So give them time to say hello and catch up a bit.

To move from the ordinary to the holy, we need something to center us, to make us fully present, not just in body but in mind, in intent. We must be able to abandon the preoccupations of the day as we shed our coats when we entered the house. We are easily distracted by problems, by events we have just gone through or anticipate experiencing. We are looking over our own shoulders and forward into the distance. We use the candlelighting to focus on this time, this place, this moment.

The use of fire to sanctify something from a meal to a sacrifice is ancient. What does a candle do? Why light little fires on the table?

Candles offer a portable form of fire, relatively safe (*relatively*, because every year homes burn because of candles left lit or knocked over). It would be a lot riskier to have a brazier on the table. Fuel was always expensive and scarce. Fire is associated with purification. Hashem appeared to Moses in exile as a burning bush that was never consumed: *I will be what I will be.* In the wandering in the desert after the flight from Egypt, the Israelites were led by a pillar of fire. Light is associated with vision and vision with truth-seeking or the truth itself. Thus light becomes truth.

A candle gives light, however limited, light that is warm and intimate, flickering. That is probably why we associate candles with romantic love, a tryst, a lover's dinner. We light candles on Shabbat to make the beginning and on most holidays we do the same. Light is for many people an appropriate image of holiness. Hence the perpetual flame that hangs in synagogues. Hence the use of a flame in burials of state. We light candles for the dead on their *yahrzeit*. We light candles on birthday cakes to mark another year completed. If Pesach falls on Shabbat, we light double sets of candles and say the appropriate blessings for both. Some families light a candle for every child.

One of my favorite forms of meditation uses a candle in a darkened room. I chant and then after a while stare into the candle flame, seeing the different colors, watching it dance and hover over the candle's body. The *Zohar* discusses the contemplation of a flame. The light without kindles the light within. We hold sparks of what is holy, what is radiant, what is precious, what is most important. The sparks get lost and buried, they are almost destroyed or, in some brutal people, snuffed out. We light candles to bring ourselves into a state where we look both inward and outward in search of peace and harmony.

I strongly recommend some additional readings at the time of the candlelighting, because you want to capture the attention of everyone at the table. You want them to be entirely present with their minds open to the ritual and the words. If you think your group will respond to meditation, try it. If there are children, however, this may not work, and it won't with many adults who simply don't have practice in clearing their minds. Do it only if you think it has a decent chance.

Lighting the candles and gazing at them, we say the blessing for the gift of light. Here is a blessing and a rough translation:

Baruch ata Adonai, eloheynu melech ha-olam, borey m'orey ha-aysh. Blessed is the source of light and fire, Ein Sof.

As someone who was legally blind for a year and lives under the threat of blindness, I appreciate light. "Let there be light," Hashem says in Genesis, and we echo those words, again and again. Let us have light, within and without. In Proverbs, teaching is compared to giving light. The teacher brings light and order.

My grandmother had given me the Hebrew name Miriam, but when I was dying at age seven of rheumatic fever, she changed my name to Marah, bitter, so Moloch ha'Moves, the angel of death, would pass over. Would not want me, would not take me. It seemed to work. That has been my Hebrew name ever since. Rabbi Zalman Schachter-Shalomi gave me the Hebrew name of Ma'ora, bringer of light, a few years ago, which he thought was far more appropriate for me. But in honor of my grandmother who gave me my religious education and was a great storyteller, I keep Marah and on formal occasions give my Hebrew name as Marah Ma'ora.

We focus on the light of the candles and it dances in our eyes, it bathes our eyes. We behold light and we praise it. Darkness, real or metaphorical, can sometimes be soothing but also frightening. There is a reason horror movies are usually set at night, not at noon. We are afraid of what may lurk in the dark, what may issue out of darkness—the beasts beyond the circle of fire. We are sometimes afraid of our own thoughts. At night as we lie in our beds, fears surge out of the dark and envelop us. If we can visualize light, if we can mentally light a candle at those moments, we may slow down our breathing and our heartbeat and quiet our minds. Fire was one of the first, if not the first, tools our distant ancestors had. Fire made food more digestible and safer to consume. We think of ourselves as more civilized for eating cooked rather than raw food. (My mother had a peasant distrust of raw foods; she was sure they caused dreadful stomach problems. She cooked vegetables until they were truly dead. My grandmother did the same.) Fire kept hungry predators away. Fire warmed and made safe. Fire enabled us to survive the deadly cold of winter. Our history as hominids and then as humans is intertwined with fire. No wonder we use it to mark the beginning of sacred time.

4
Blessings

At traditional points in the haggadah, particular blessings are spoken in Hebrew, but if so, I strongly recommend that you provide a transliteration. It is not fair to assume everyone or even every Jew has a working knowledge of Hebrew. The women may have grown up in a tradition where only the boys are bar mitzvahed. Those who did study may never have used what Hebrew was forced into them when they were twelve. My own grandmother considered herself ignorant although she knew four languages, because she—a rabbi's daughter—had never been taught Hebrew. The women prayed in Yiddish.

Consider also if you have invited someone with no religious training in their background or guests who are not Jewish, how meaningful the seder could possibly be to them in gibberish. Unless everyone is fluent in Hebrew, English in the haggadah will have to do the work of carrying the evening's *kavanah*—intention—forward.

The Hebrew is sonorous. If you have provided a transliteration, everyone can recite the blessings with the leader. The Hebrew is also traditionally masculine. I alternate blessings in the masculine and the feminine. You might also consider nonsexist alternatives such as the blessings that Marcia Falk has written. Or create your own.

I'll go through the seder in the traditional order but you should remember that fifteen parts is an arbitrary number. Some parts get counted and some parts don't. Try to make sure everybody has a copy of the haggadah you are using. Of course, two people can look on a copy together, but it really works out for the best if you provide a copy for everyone who can read. Now, the order of the seder (*seder* means "order") did not come down from Mount Sinai on stone tablets. It's been added to and changed around for a couple thousand years, so feel free to leave out any parts that don't touch you. I often skip the second handwashing, as it interrupts the seder and sometimes makes a mess.

If guests have never attended a seder before, make them feel welcome and state clearly that they can ask questions. If they do and you are leading the seder, don't take it upon yourself to answer all questions. Have others at the table share that labor. It will encourage whoever answers to formulate what that particular ritual could mean.

What you are doing for most of the people at your seder is mixing the familiar with what should be somewhat different, for this night should be different from other nights, and your seder should be at least a little different from all other seders. If we don't shake things up a bit, we become stuck in our habits, enslaved by rituals we no longer experience as more than routine. If you don't change your seder, you will not be fulfilling the commandment to feel as if each one of us personally was a slave in Egypt and then liberated. It is vitally important to alter a few passages or activities each year. Sometimes I have been guilty of failing to do this, because I was traveling too much, because I didn't start in time to work on my haggadah that year. Whatever the reason, the result was a less moving and less engaging experience.

If you have invited a guest to your seder who is used to all the traditional readings and long sections in Hebrew, warn them beforehand that they should expect something different. If they are not comfortable with that, let them know you understand and perhaps they will find a seder more to their liking. Don't make the person used to a traditional seder feel unwelcome, but let them know it will not be what they are accustomed to. When I have failed to do this, I have sometimes understood that my guests were appalled at not experiencing what they had anticipated.

1 . KIDDUSH

After the blessing of the candles, given in the last chapter, we say a blessing over the first cup of wine (more likely a glass, of course). In the masculine Hebrew it is:

Baruch ata Adonai eloheynu melech ha-olam borey pri hagafen.

In the feminine it is:

Bruchah at shekinah eloheynu ruach ha-olam boreyt prit hagafen.
Blessed is the Eternal One, spirit of the world, who gives us the fruit of the vine.

Why do I include the feminine form of every blessing? In Hebrew, unlike English, every noun has gender. If we use only the male terms for Hashem, inevitably we come to imagine "Him" as masculine. Yet there is in Judaism a recognition that the Eternal is without attributes of male or female. In kabbalah, when the Ein Sof moves into matter, into actuality, what was without boundaries or attributes becomes both male and female. The Shekinah is the female manifestation of Hashem. If women are to be truly Jews, then we, too, are the image of what is holy. So I alternate in my own seder between the masculine and feminine forms of the blessings.

Then we give the blessing that begins every holiday:

Brukhah at Shekinah
eloheynu malkat ha-olam,
she-heh-khi-a-tanu
v'kimatanu, v'higi'atanu
la-z'man ha-zeh.

That is the traditional blessing rendered into the feminine form. The following is not a translation but a blessing in English:

Blessed is the force of life that brings us to this year's spring and to this renewal of our search for freedom. Let us be glad that we are alive to reach this season.

Or you might like this one:

We are grateful to come together to celebrate the liberation of our people and the renewal of all the earth in the spring light and gathering warmth. Let us appreciate the life that flows through us and the life we share with all beings on this earth.

or:

We have arrived at a time in the year when everything is growing and opening up. Let us always try to enjoy what is good that the turning year brings us and let us taste each new fruit and vegetable of the season as if we had never eaten it before. Let us experience the people and events of our lives as if they were new to us.

I have written and used these blessings and others throughout the years. Since every haggadah provides the masculine forms of the blessings in Hebrew, from now on I'll just give the feminine. I like to sing the Shehechiyanu, then say a blessing in English. The Shehechiyanu opens every season and every holiday. You can also use it whenever you taste or do something for the first time, at least the first time that year. It marks the passage of time and the entry of a new season marked off from what came before it. Time is one of the elements that renders the blessings, the candle-lighting, the wine drinking so important. We are marking sacred time as opposed to mundane time. But we are also just "taking our time."

Time is often the thing of which we now have the least. We are overly busy. Time is the thing we *lose* and mind losing. We *steal* time for lovemaking, for eating something slowly and relishing it, for talking with friends, with children, with parents. If we *waste* time, we don't get it back except by stinting sleep or giving up something we wanted or needed to do. We *spend* time. We're bankrupts of time, but there is no way to recoup our losses. Although the eternal is timeless, our time is short and it moves ever more quickly. So, to set aside time to heal ourselves, to explore Judaism, to renew ourselves and resolve how to live a more useful and less self-centered life, to be a better person, is not easy. Few Jews beyond the Orthodox really take a Shabbat—but, oh, how we need it, not to sit still in a dark room but to restore ourselves and knit our closest ties stronger. We must forcefully *take* the time for holidays that are holy days. Without time, we cannot make them holy. We cannot make them meaningful.

So lest we bring with us all the daily buzz of the media and our worries, our anxieties, our vanities, our fantasies, all the flies that swarm our minds, we have ways of ending distraction and entering into focused time. Blessings are for those who bless, not for the Eternal. They are ways of calling attention to something so that we more fully experience it. Noticing what apples taste like. Noticing what irises smell like. Noticing the voice of someone you love. Noticing the way snow clings to the bark of a tree. *Noticing:* paying attention, for attention is something you *pay* as you *spend* time. We speak of these things as if they were losses, but if you truly concentrate on a blessing, if you experience what the blessing is celebrating, it is you who are at least momentarily blessed.

We drink the first cup of wine now. We might want to do it while remembering all those who have not been freed of their burdens but who suffer under them. We might talk about those burdens, the various kinds of slavery, the women and children who are bought and sold for the pleasure of others and for sexual tourists, women and children who die young because of their slavery. We might talk about the slavery of those who work in sweatshops here and abroad. We might talk of those whom poverty enslaves, who cannot get the education they need because the schools are useless and there is no one to encourage them, because they cannot afford a real education. We might talk of *agunot,* women whose marriages have ended but who are trapped because they cannot get the ex-husband to become fully "ex" by granting them a *get.* We might talk of those who live in repressive regimes in fear, or those who are unlucky enough to live in a place where a war is fought with their lives in danger and their means of making a living destroyed.

2 . URCHATZ

There is no blessing over the washing of hands that immediately follows the Shehechiyanu. That is reserved for the second cere-monial washing of hands just before the meal is served. It might be interesting to ask why we wash our hands symbolically, and why we do it twice. In part, the rabbis who created the traditional haggadah over centuries were trying to provoke the interest, the curiosity of children (you shall tell your children, Exodus keeps saying) and also to provoke questions. The seder does not want us to be passive participants. So why do we wash our hands rather than our faces or our feet or our teeth? What is it about the agency of our hands we are being asked to remember, to experi-ence, to consider? At some seders, people wash one another's hands. That is more mutual and cooperative, but it might not give you the space to contemplate the products and activities of your own hands. Now we always wash our hands before we eat—I hope—if we don't want to carry germs to our mouths. But passing around a basin of water and towel has little to do with actually cleaning our hands in a useful way. Rather it is an announcement that we are purifying ourselves for what we are about to perform. It sets off this meal from other meals in our daily lives or on social occasions—having friends over, eating with family or colleagues, Thanksgiving, other events when a feast is consumed.

In some communities, only the leaders of the seders wash their hands. But we all wash our hands at my seder to signify our equality. Everybody reads from the haggadah and thus shares in the creation of the seder, so we all purify ourselves by the symbolic dipping of our hands in the water and the real drying of them on a passed towel. It is a symbolic purifying. We are washing away the mundane, the trivial, the imperfections of our days.

The traditional explanation for why there are four cups of wine is that there are four promises that Hashem gives the people in Exodus: "I will free you from the Egyptians." "I will deliver you from bondage." "I will redeem you with an outstretched arm." "I will take you to be my people and I will be your God." Over the years, dozens of other explanations of the importance of the number four in the Haggadah have emerged. There are lots of "fours" in the seder—four questions, four children. You should consider what *you* want to bless at each of the four cups. If you are using a haggadah that is particularly suitable for your family or group, maybe you want to use the blessings it provides. But you may want to change one or more of the blessings to represent the concerns of your group or the particular year. For instance, if a natural disaster has occurred, if something is going on in the Middle East, as always, if our country has started a war or gone into one, if there is a particular plague or ecological disaster that has surfaced, you may want to direct some part of your seder toward that.

3. KARPAS

The next blessing is over Karpas. In the feminine God language
it is:

> *Brukhah Yah Shekinah*
> *eloheynu malkat ha'olam,*
> *borah p'rit ha adamah.*

Blessed is the Eternal One who creates the fruit of the earth.

or something like this:

*Blessed is the force of life, the strength of farm workers who plant and
harvest fruit, grains, and vegetables from the earth. The fields declare that
winter is past, the rains have come, the flowers appear and cover the earth.
The season of maximum birdsong has come. These greens represent nature
and our own energies reborn.*

There is a lot more in chapter 6 about Karpas and the salt water in
which we dip it.

4. YACHATZ

Next the middle matzoh of the three is broken into a larger piece
that will be the afikomen and a smaller piece that goes back into
the napkin or matzoh cover. Remember about these artifacts of
the seder—such as the seder plate or the matzoh cover—that it is
nice to have them. Still, I have been at seders with gorgeous silver

cups and embroidered matzoh covers that were boring and mean-ingless. I have been to seders where a kitchen towel was the mat-zoh cover and the glasses were jam jars, yet the seder was one to remember for its fervor and energy. You want a seder to be as beautiful as you can make it, but energy should go into the ritual itself and not into its accoutrements. I read an account of a Pesach held secretly in a ditch in a concentration camp in which they managed to bake one matzoh and share it—no wine, no food, no candles. Yet it was truly an extraordinary Pesach.

5 . MAGGID

Just before you get to the tale, you need to pass the wine and have everybody pour a little into their glasses so that they will have some for the Ten Plagues. This is because you already drank the first cup and you don't get to pour the second cup until after the Maror (see page 50). So you take a little at the beginning of the Maggid and don't drink any of it. It is for making drops only, when the plagues are recounted.

Just before we wash our hands and then eat the bitter herbs, the Maror, we drink the second cup of wine.

6 . RACHATZA

We wash our hands (again symbolically) by pouring water over them or dipping them into a basin passed from hand to hand as the blessing is said:

Bruchah Yah Shekinah Ruach ha-olam asher kideshanu bemitzvotav vetzivanu al netilat yadayim.

You could say something like this:

Blessed is the Spirit of the Universe who gave us the commandment to wash our hands—to experience the cool water on our hands in silence, thinking about our hands and what they have done and what they must do. Think about all the hands of others who do for you here and around the world, who mine the minerals in your car, your phone, your computer, your kitchenware, who create the cloth and sew your clothing, who do all the labor of the world. Who pick up after you and tend your sicknesses.

7 . MATZI

Then comes the double blessing for the matzoh. First comes the regular blessing for bread:

Blessed be the One who brings forth bread from the earth.
Bruchah Yah Shekinah ruach ha-olam ha-motzi lechem min ha-aretz.
Bruchah Yah Shekinah ruach ha-olam asher kideshanu bemitzvotav vetzivanu al achilat matzoh.

Let us bless this moment when we choose to eat matzoh. Our ancestors, in their haste to be free, had no choice. It was matzoh or nothing. For so many people in the world today, they must eat whatever they can, if they have anything to eat at all. Let us bless those who work to end hunger, and bless all those who suffer it.

or:

Now we eat the matzoh to remember our ancestors and reexperience their choice. This is the bread of affliction and of liberation.

These English blessings are just suggestions to inspire your own.

8 . MATZOH

At this point the top matzoh is taken from its cover. The remaining portion of the middle matzoh is passed along and everybody eats a little bit of each. Check out chapter 11 on matzoh for explanation and discussion.

9 . MAROR

We bless the bitter herbs before we eat them. Chapter 12 discusses Maror.

Bruchah Yah Shekinah ruach ha-olam asher kideshanu bemitzvotav vetzivanu al achilat maror.

After a while, even if your Hebrew is rusty or weak, you get pretty good at shifting genders. It's easy once you figure out the formula.

We eat the bitter herbs now to remember the suffering of our ancestors in slavery. We eat the bitter herbs to remember our own pain and the stifling of our best selves. We eat bitter herbs in solidarity with all those who suffer now under all kinds of oppression and fear and imprisonment, whose freedom has been taken or never enjoyed to begin with.

1 0 . K O R E C H

Now we make a Hillel sandwich of matzoh and bitter herbs. Some people use the Chazeret here instead of the Maror. Many people add Charoset to the sandwich.

1 1 . S H U L H A N O R E K H

The meal is served. There are many recipes in chapter 19, "The Feast," if you don't already have your own favorites or if you've gotten tired of them.

1 2 . T Z A F U N

After dessert, the afikomen drama (or comedy of errors) ensues. This is discussed in chapter 11. When the children—or whoever is allowed to search for it—find the afikomen and get their reward, if you do it that way; or after the afikomen is ransomed by the child or children who stole it and they get a ransom from the leader of the seder, then we move on.

Get everyone seated again and get them back into order. This may take a little doing, as probably everyone has been jolly and relaxed and talkative during the meal. They are stuffed now and maybe a bit sleepy. I think it's appropriate to offer coffee or tea with dessert, just before the afikomen is returned and everyone has a little symbolic bite of it. It's important to wake people up for the last part of the haggadah. While shorter than the first, it is important and you want people's attention.

1 3 . B A R E C H

Christians say grace before meals. We express our gratitude after we have eaten. We are certainly happier after we have feasted than we were after the long first section of the haggadah. So now you pour the third cup of wine and say or sing some birkat ha-mazon—grace. There are many birkat ha-mazons for you to choose from. The haggadah you're using probably provides one or you can make your own or choose one of the many contemporary ones.

You drink your wine now, but you may want to keep some in your glass if you use drops of wine to mark the death camps and concentration camps, discussed in chapter 20. If you don't, then drink it all. At this point in my seder, we bless all those who have struggled for freedom, those who fought back, those who resisted, and those who fight and resist right now.

Many people use this section to remember the Holocaust. Chapter 20 suggests one way to deal with this. You probably know others. If family members have stories they did not share during the Maggid, this would be a fine time to do so.

Then comes the cup of Eliyahu, the opening of the door, and the singing of "Eliyahu ha-navi"—Eliyahu the prophet. After that, many of us raise the cup of Miriam. If you wish, you can pour some fresh water in everyone's glass and drink some water—not a bad idea at this juncture. See chapter 21 for suggestions on Miriam.

1 4 . H A L L E L

We are now in the concluding section when we pour the fourth glass of wine. If you are using a traditional format, you recite some psalms. Most people do a lot of singing. Then you drink the fourth cup. The seder has moved from memories of slavery and our history into the present and here we look to the future. I like a blessing here that looks forward. There are many possibilities:

Bless those who work for a future that will bring further liberation to at least some of those who suffer in the present. Bless those who will bring us further understanding and enlightenment in our daily lives. Bless those who will create in words and in music and in art and dance visions that increase our empathy and our joy. Bless those who bring peace between people and between nations. Bless those who repair some little bit of the world for our children and our children's children's children.

1 5 . N I R T Z A H

There are suggestions for concluding the seder in chapter 22. Throughout, do not be afraid to improvise your blessings or create suitable ones for your particular circle of friends, your family, your time and place. New blessings are something we truly need, if we are to feel the holiness and beauty of the world and of our heritage. There's nothing wrong with the traditional blessings if they move you, but you have to feel what you are saying for it to be more than mumbling. One possibility is to ask people at the table to say a blessing on the spot; or you could ask individuals to prepare a short (and ask them to keep it short) blessing for a particular point in the seder. Make sure they understand the context. It's another way of involving people in the seder.

*W*ine is ancient. Until recently, it was thought not to be as old as beer, first brewed five thousand years ago. Wine was first fermented, it was believed, in Mesopotamia: first came pottery, then wine. However, *Vitis vinifera sylvestis,* the original wine grape that still produces 99 percent of the world's wine, grows wild in the Caucasus Mountains. Ancient jars found in Iran have pushed back the date of wine in the Middle East to seventy-four hundred years ago, older than the first ale.

The origins of wine are still being actively explored. The Noah Hypothesis takes wine back into the Neolithic period. Modern Armenia, Azerbaijan, and Georgia seem the most probable sites for the first cultivation of wine. Excavations near Yerevan in Armenia and Tbilisi in Georgia show continuous occupation going well back into Neolithic times. Georgia today still produces more than sixty kinds of wine from five hundred varietals. To grow grapes for wine takes a lot of work: vines have to be planted, cultivated to keep the weeds down, in many areas irrigated, pruned, protected from bugs and bacteria, and harvested at the right time. Vines don't really produce until they are five or six years old. Yet slowly but surely, wherever they could be grown around the Black Sea, the Caspian, and the Mediterranean, grapes were grown and some kind of wine produced.

Much ancient wine was probably, like contemporary Mogen David, sweet and rather syrupy. It was full of additives to preserve it—a memory of which comes out of every glass of retsina you might guzzle in a Greek restaurant—or to render it palatable by flavoring or sweetening it. Terebinth was often added to ancient wines grown in the region of what is now Israel. Remember Absalom, the rebellious son of David? He died when his hair was caught in the branches of a terebinth tree. The sap is resinous and was in common use to keep wine from spoiling.

The first thing to decide for your seder is what kind of wine to serve. I myself am partial to the sweet kosher wines made from Concord grapes because they create a sense of nostalgia in me and in my partner, Ira Wood. But many of our guests have revolted and bring kosher wines that are dry and aspiring to resemble normal table wine. I have never tasted one that was all that good, but they pass. We also provide grape juice for children and for those who abstain from alcohol. Children, by the way, if they are allowed a little bit, always like the sweet kosher wines. I know I did. Concord grapes are presumably a cross between *Vitis vinifera* and *Vitis labrusca*, the notorious fox grape that grows wild here—and foxes do eat it, as I have witnessed. According to Philip J. Pauly, the breeder of the Concord grape, it was superior because it is not "tainted" by its Semitic—as he believed— origins. How ironic, then, that around 1900 the Concord became the preferred grape for kosher wine.

Water was probably drinkable in the ancient land of Palestine, but for much of our history it was dangerous. As populations grew, they kept animals whose manure leaked into shallow wells, as did human waste. Water was polluted, and without refrigeration you could not drink fruit juice, and you could not drink milk except right from the cow, sheep, or goat, whatever you had. You turned milk into yogurt or cheese or butter. Before the invention of canning in the nineteenth century, you fermented fruit juices into some kind of alcoholic beverage. In the more recent past, you learned how to distill it into something more potent and far easier to transport and keep without spoilage. Fruit, if it did not become wine, became hard liquor. If you live in a place where storms—high winds, hurricanes, nor'easters, tornadoes—knock out your electricity, you learn quickly how many of the foods and liquids we are used to can turn bad and inedible, even sickening.

The Egyptians mostly drank ale. The yeast that causes wine to ferment is the same yeast that creates beer, ale, and date wine to ferment (date wine was immensely popular in Mesopotamia) and that causes bread to rise. Often wine was mixed into a grain compound like barley in order to make it ferment. Wine had a classier reputation, even in ancient times. Wine has a sacral significance in much of the area where it is commonly drunk. If you grow grapes, there is something strange and miraculous in the process by which they turn into a beverage that can make you happy, tearful, violent, silly, or just feeling special. A god of whatever intoxicates you is common among polytheistic peoples.

My grandmother made wine out of apples, berries, vegetables, whatever would ferment. When I was fifteen we moved into a much larger house than the tiny one I grew up in. In the backyard was a sour cherry tree, and my mother immediately began making wine from it. I wouldn't say it was good, but it was what we had, and I certainly drank it with pleasure. My mother would not drink beer or hard liquor, but she would drink wine, for she had grown up with it, of course. Wine is food for many people, something that is part of a meal. My grandmother always told me that wine was good for you, and now it seems that science agrees with her. Of course, she also said that schmaltz—chicken fat—was good for you, which I guess is true if you live in a shtetl in a cold climate where famine always looms. I use chicken or goose fat for holidays, but otherwise I cook with olive oil. If you want to render your own fat, see chapter 18, "Chicken Soup."

In Jewish tradition, formal and informal, wine is associated with happy times, with joy, with weddings, with Shabbat, with Passover. It is not, for instance, traditional to drink wine at or after funerals. This particular night, we are bidden to drink four cups of wine: two before the meal, two afterward. It is up to you how full you make your glass, but once you have poured it, you should drink it all at the moment you are supposed to. There is a blessing every time and whoever is leading the seder will raise her or his glass. If you are worried about drinking too much, just don't pour a lot into your glass when the bottles come to you. But a little giddy feeling is not frowned at tonight. When I was a young adult, I used to fill my glass and drink it all down. Now that I am the responsible one at the head of the table, I only take half a glass each time. I don't want to forget anything or lose my place. We pass my haggadah around and everybody who is willing reads, but I make sure the ritual goes along smoothly. We have to remain reasonable enough to experience the meaning of Pesach and to feel its power to encourage us to change and liberate ourselves. Unlike Purim, where careless wine drinking is part of the festivities, at Pesach the glasses are counted and limited.

The association in Judaism of wine and joy, wine and celebration is widespread and deep-seated. This is a poem written as part of a wedding ceremony, but it exemplifies what wine means.

The wine

Red is the body's own deep song,
the color of lips, of our busy
organs, heart and stomach and lungs,
the color of our roused genitals,
the color of tongues and the flag of our blood.

Red is the loudest color
and the most secret
lurking inside the clothes' cocoon,
baked in the dark of the nightly bed
like coals shimmering in a stove.

It is the hot color, the active
that dances into your eye leaping,
that goads and pricks you
with its thorn of fire,
that shouts and urges and commands.

But red coils in the wineglass
head into tail like a dozing cat
whose eyes have shut but who purrs still
the pleasure of your hand, whose
warmth gently loosens the wine's aroma

so it rises like a perfumed ghost
inside the chambers of your nose.
In the mouth wine opens
its hundred petals like a damask rose
and then subside, swallowed to afterglow.

In the wine press of the bed
of all the salty flows of our bodies,
the heat of our love ferments
our roundness into the midnight red
flowering of the wine

that can make drunken and make warm
that can comfort and quicken the sluggish
that can ease the weary body into sleep
that can frame the dark bread and cheese
into feast, that can celebrate

and sing through the wine of the body,
its own bright blood that rushes
to every cranny and cove of the flesh
and dark of the bone, the joy in love
that is the wine of life.

At festivals and every Shabbat, we bless wine. This separates wine that is consecrated for the holidays from ordinary wine drunk simply as a pleasant beverage with the meal. Why bless wine? Why do we set off this time as something special? Because it is chosen time. It is time we want to keep apart from regular work and play, from watching TV and surfing the Internet, apart from chatting with friends and shopping at the mall and doing laundry. Therefore we bless the candles and bless the wine, bringing ceremony into our lives to make a given block of time sacred.

Why wine? Although some people use grape juice, wine is ancient and traditional. It has seemed to people since they started fermenting grapes intentionally that something wonderful and unexpected happens. Sharing wine, like sharing food, is a ritual that brings people together and often changes their mood and leads them to socialize. Wine for Passover is usually made in a different way: instead of adding the usual yeast to cause fermentation, months before the holiday grape juice is exposed to air so that natural and wild yeasts enter to convert grape juice into wine.

In the Christian Mass, wine represents blood, a symbolism that is alien to the seder. Each glass we drink is consecrated to something. We are remembering and holding in our minds a particular event or idea as we drink that glass. Each glass is different in its intent. There are two points in many haggadahs in which the wine may stand for blood. The first time is when the Ten Plagues are recited and a drop of wine is cast on the plate for each plague. The other time is in the second half of the seder, after the meal and after the third cup is poured, when in a number of haggadahs the Holocaust is remembered, as in chapter 20.

I want to return to the question of why wine is important. If the matzoh represents essence, wine conjures up change. Drinking it may change your mental state. Change starts with the grapes, bunches of them hanging on the vine. The grapevine in nature is lush and wandering. If allowed to grow freely, it will climb a large tree. But vines for wine are pruned and pruned again, restrained, forced into shape. Often they are trained on wires. So wine begins from a change to the vine, a forced change in which the vine cannot be free. Change is often forced upon us from outside. We often act as if we expect our lives to putter along much as they have. We make plans for next week, next month, next year, for college for ourselves or our children or grandchildren, for buying houses, for retirement. We plant trees, fully expecting to see them mature to bear fruit or to grow eighty feet tall.

But change sometimes comes unbidden, often unexpectedly, and only those with the willingness to believe it is happening and the willingness to do what must be done to survive the change will move on in their lives. A hurricane plows through Florida or Louisiana and flattens houses, destroys whole communities, leaves behind wreckage instead of homes, businesses, shops, schools, orchards, bridges. A tornado cuts a narrower path but leaves total devastation wherever it touches down. A tsunami carries away entire villages. Fires sweep down and communities turn to ash. Governments change and repression mounts. Jews in Germany often resisted leaving. "Move out of my beautiful house? Sell off cheap this business my grandfather founded? Leave my community? Uproot my family and discard everything we have enjoyed and built here? This is where I grew up; my friends are here, my livelihood. Here my parents and grandparents are buried. Here my child goes to school." So they could not persuade themselves to leave and were murdered.

Wine embodies change. It is the fruit of the vine, as we sing in our blessing, but what a changed fruit. Grapes have no choice as to whether they become table fruit, raisins, or wine, and some-

times people have little choice. But tonight we praise our ancestors who willingly changed, who walked out of slavery, who
fought their way out of whatever oppression they were enduring.

Two of the cups of wine are poured and drunk in the first
and lengthier part of the seder, before the meal. Two cups follow
the meal. The meaning of each of the cups varies from haggadah
to haggadah. Choose a haggadah that speaks to you. If you
walk into a Jewish bookstore, you will find probably sixty different ones. There are thousands; women's haggadahs, liberation
haggadahs, ultra-traditional haggadahs, vegetarian haggadahs,
antiwar haggadahs, Zionist haggadahs, haggadahs that use traditional songs and those that incorporate other music, often spirituals like "Let My People Go," "Go Tell It on the Mountain," and "O
Freedom." You can download a haggadah from the Internet,
where there are plenty. You can then print out as many copies as
you need. Once you have picked your haggadah, don't hesitate
to play around with it—to add, to subtract, to find other readings
you want to include. *The important thing is not to touch all bases, but to
create a telling, a ritual that engages everyone at the table.*

As I remarked in chapter 4, "Blessings," each of the four cups
has a traditional association, the four statements in Exodus. Even
if you recite a standard blessing, you are free to dedicate that cup
or glass of wine to whomever or whatever you choose. Think of it
as a toast, not in the jolly, casual sense, but as a way of honoring
whatever you feel is appropriate at that point in the seder. You
might want to dedicate that first glass to something or someone
appropriate to the changing of the seasons; you might want to
honor some hero or heroine of the past at the second cup; you
might want to dedicate the third glass to someone in the present

or the past who resisted tyranny or oppression; you might want to dedicate the fourth glass to something having to do with hope for the future.

In any case, the meaning of each of the four cups is yours to choose: what is traditional, what your haggadah suggests, or what you and those who are making this seder with you find most meaningful and appropriate. This is your ritual: do not be afraid to shape it in ways that resonate for you and for your guests. You can also ask four people, well beforehand, to create blessing or toast to go with a cup. Ask them to write something short but meaningful to them and, you hope, to the group. Why should you do all the work? Get your people involved.

6
Karpas and Salt Water

*T*here is some overlap between the various greens used in the seder. Karpas is usually parsley or celery. Parsley and celery are close relatives botanically, to the point where in some languages the same word is used for both. I prefer parsley as Karpas because it often overwinters in my garden, with a little help from mulching with straw or leaves, so that its sprouting really is a sign of spring. Being a biennial, it is good only for a while in the spring, up until it starts to flower and make seed. You can prolong its usefulness by cutting back the flowers as soon as they begin to form. Plain-leaved parsley is hardier than curly parsley, but both will survive the winter if the weather is not unusually fierce and if they are mulched.

Some instructions say that a potato or a radish can be used. That's even less satisfactory than celery, but the reason they got on the approved list is that Pesach can come far too early in Poland and Russia, for instance, for there to be much in the way of greens to use as Karpas.

Karpas sits on the seder plate as a sprig or two, but a heap of it waits to the side to be passed around the table with a vessel of salty water so that everyone can dip the parsley into the salt water and then eat it. Wash the parsley carefully beforehand, as parsley loves to hide bits of sand or loam, especially if you are using the curly kind. Dry it so that it takes up the salty water. (Not only is it disconcerting to find sand in your teeth as you chew the parsley, but the salty water is not inviting if there are flecks of something in it.)

Many haggadahs start with an evocation of spring. When the holiday of Pesach originated, Nisan was the first month of the year. In many ways that made perfect sense. The agricultural year does begin in the spring. Pesach is a renewal—of our sense of what it means to be a Jew, of our reconnection to our history, of our sense of what we need to change in our lives and in the world at large, just as nature begins to open buds and sprout little leaflets, to unfurl fern fronds, to call the birds back north, to replace dead grass with new growth. It is the season of mating; it is the season of birth. So parsley is a potent symbol of the greening of spring. Every living thing is growing once again. Every creature and tree is awake. Everything is moving forward, intentionally or blindly. The rains come. Streams and rivers swell. Lambs and calves, kittens and puppies are born. We talk about liberation in the personal and societal and political sense on Pesach, but there is also a liberation of the season, especially if you live in the northern areas where winter is real and prolonged. Spring is a true liberation—from cabin fever, from being shut inside. It is a liberation to walk, to dig, to garden, to play, to bike, walk, or run. We are let loose into nature.

But nothing is ever simple, so we take the Karpas and dip it in salt water to remind us of sorrow in the midst of simple joy and to remember the tears shed by our ancestors and by others hard put to survive: to call into our consciousness tears shed by those around the world whose homes are bombed or burned, whose land is taken from them, whose families are torn apart, whose husband or wife, brother or sister, father or mother, grandparents or children are maimed or killed or imprisoned or whom some government causes to simply disappear. Spring renews the earth, but the sparrow that returns may not be the one that left the previous fall. Our lives have rhythms of what returns and what does not return. We come to the seder every year, but we may not all be there. Friends move away, friends die, parents die, children leave home; even children may die. People we cherished are one way or another lost to us. There are empty places not only for Eliyahu, but empty places for those we have lost. We dip the symbol of spring and renewal into the symbol of pain and regret, the salty water that is akin to our blood and our sweat. We are largely made of slightly salty water; it never hurts to remember that.

Salt waters

It is a bowl of tears on the table
into which we drip the parsley,
into which we dip the egg.

It is a miniature ocean on the table,
salt as the Sea of Reeds through
which they were to pass

not to safety (never safety)
but to where they were promised
they would if they chose be free.

It is the salt water of our sweat
pressed through our skin
as the body labors, for we are bidden

not only to rest on the seventh day
but to work on the others, and the brain
too in its fever of creation exudes

salt like the sea, salt like our blood
salt like the waters of the womb
the salt of regret and the salt of effort.

Salt is one of those everyday things we seldom think about unless we are trying to avoid it. Too much salt and you may suffer high blood pressure. Too little and your strength will diminish. Salt regulates the balance of fluids in the body, enables nerve impulses to work and muscles to react and move. None and your food is not palatable and you will grow weaker and weaker and finally die. Most of us eat meat and fish. Everybody eats vegetables, grains, and fruit. But we don't generally eat rocks. We may consume dolomite ground up as a food supplement. But the rock we eat every day is sodium chloride.

Bread and salt are the signs of hospitality to the stranger, whom we are bidden to welcome and treat kindly, for we were strangers in the land of Egypt, as the Amidah reminds us. Besides evaporation at salt springs or the seaside, salt is mined as rocks or crystals. The crystals look like quartz, but if you lick them they are salty. I used to have a beautiful crystal of salt from a mine twelve hundred feet under Detroit.

Before refrigeration, salt was one of the primary means of preserving food. If a family slaughtered a sheep in the fall—because how could they feed it all winter?—they might not eat it all at once. So they would preserve the meat by using salt. Back in the mid-'60s, I was traveling with a companion in a battered VW bug on a country road in the Peloponnesus when a middle-aged man ran out into the road and flagged us down. It was Greek Easter. They had killed a lamb, cooked it on a spit in the fireplace, and eaten it, the whole family—parents, children, grandparents, an aunt, and an uncle—until they were full. There was still lamb left over, so they invited us in and fed it to us with potatoes roasted in the ashes. It was excellent. Their desire was hospitality to strangers, but their problem was they had no way to preserve meat. Whatever lore had previously existed had been lost. It did not occur to them to smoke or salt it. Salt also preserves cabbage as sauerkraut and cucumbers as pickles. Salt is essential to a lot of cheese making—a means originally of preserving milk.

Salt may take on water in the summer humidity and become difficult to pour or even to shake out, but it does not deteriorate. Salt does not oxidize—one reason it's a preservative. It dehydrates meat or fish. You use salt to draw the extra fluid out of zucchini for certain uses and to remove the bitter fluid from eggplants before cooking. Salt is often part of drying—for instance, if you are drying slices of tomato. Salt desiccates.

Salt was so important that which side a country might join in a war was sometimes determined by the salt trade. A case in point is Bavaria's habit of allying with France against Austria. According to Mark Kurlansky in *Salt: A World History,* Venice and Genoa had vast trading empires based on the salt trade. Caravans crossed the Sahara carrying salt one way and gold the other. Seizing an enemy's supply of salt was a way to weaken them, since they could not preserve their food. General Sherman used that tactic against the South. Salt has been mined for thousands of years, but salt licks were important long before people appeared. All vertebrates need salt. Salt licks have always drawn both predators and prey.

We Jews seem to need a lot of salt, or think we do, at least we Ashkenazi. We like salty herring; we like pickled tomatoes and cucumbers, pastrami and corned beef, salted and smoked fish, especially lox—or nova in the less salty style—sturgeon, whitefish, sable, even preserved tongue. Salt is one of the traditional vices of our culture.

No pain, no gain, you say when you exercise, and the salty water into which we dip the Karpas may also remind us that sometimes out of sorrow and pain comes a kind of strength. Would we have become a nation if we had not sojourned in Egypt and been forced into slavery? That could have broken the people, but without that agony might not the Israelites have assimilated and lost their identity, as so many of the groups mentioned in Genesis have? If we use the adversity we have endured in a way that strengthens us, we can move beyond victimization. We can have the ability to try to change the conditions, the situations that confine and oppress us. A completely happy person may be static. If all your needs are met, why change? You sometimes see children who grew up in very happy homes with wonderful parents reluctant to mature, to go out on their own. Why leave home when home is almost perfect? Not that we need to be miserable in order to mature, but some dissatisfaction surely is a goad. Serious pain, real oppression can cripple us or inspire rebellion and a search for freedom.

Still, dipping into salt water is a weird-enough activity to inspire the third of the four traditional questions. Not that we don't dip: we dip taco chips into guacamole; we dip pita bread into hummus. Fast-food franchises have made millions from dipping chicken fingers and pizza. We dip bread into soup or stew. But we don't usually take a vegetable and dip it in salty water.

Some commentators associate salt water with amniotic fluid and the notion of being reborn or renewing life. Others see the dipping of the Karpas in salt water as a means to evoke the night of the first Passover, when the Israelites were bidden to dip hyssop twigs in the blood of the Paschal lamb and to mark their doorways with that blood, so that Moloch Ha-Moves, the Angel of Death—my grandmother would mention him with a sign to avert evil—would pass over and leave the firstborn of the slaves alive and kill only the firstborn of the Egyptians. These commentaries usually cite hyssop as something found in the Middle East. I can find hyssop by walking twenty feet out my door. It is a perennial, perfectly hardy here on Cape Cod; I always have hyssop and anise hyssop in my herb garden. Both are beautiful, vigorous plants with many flowers that bees love. Still, there would not be enough of it leafed out by Pesach to use as Karpas.

Salt preserves, so think about what we want to preserve out of our heritage, out of the experience of slavery, out of persecution and revolt and escape. Once when he had finally come to a poetry reading of mine, my brother asked me, *"Why do you write about those old unhappy experiences from our family? Why would people want to come and hear about them?"* So we might ask ourselves, Why should we remember slavery in Egypt so long ago? Why remember the Exodus? This is worth talking about at your seder.

Anyone who grew up on the bland food of the '50s and early '60s probably is a snob about parsley. It was the only herb used in most homes, unless the mother retained some attachment to her ethnic roots. Cooks mistrusted other herbs, and few Americans grew them. Parsley was not something you ate. It was something that arrived on your plate like a paper ruffle on the end bone of a leg of lamb, and you put it aside. Most people would no more eat the garnish of parsley than they would chew the colored umbrella stuck in their rum drink in a Polynesian-themed restaurant.

But parsley is essential to many cuisines, including French, Italian, and Greek, that make abundant use of herbs. Parsley often joins in fines herbes, or in a bouquet garni, or as a *persillade*—a sautéed mix of finely chopped parsley and garlic. It appears in Italian cooking mixed with lemon zest and garlic. It joins with basil or mint in Greek recipes. It's one taste that belongs to Ashkenazi, Sephardic, and Mizraki cooking alike.

Eat your parsley: not only is it tasty but it's good for you. It contains beta-carotene, vitamin C, and apiol—used in medications for kidney problems—as well as natural antihistamines. Its medical properties have been known for thousands of years, and it was part of general herbal lore everyplace where it grew naturally or in cultivation. Parsley tea is still used as a diuretic.

Of my four acres of property, part of the land is wild and about half an acre is under intense cultivation. I start my first seeds indoors in mid-February. By mid-March, we are planting peas and beginning to put out the hardy seedlings under old milk cartons that serve as mini greenhouses—lettuce, spring Chinese cabbage, bok choi, broccoli, red cabbage, and parsley. Spring to me is well under way when my city friends are whining whether it will ever arrive. By "spring" they mean weather in which they can comfortably toss a ball around, go out with only a sweater, eat lunch on a park bench. By "spring" I mean that the ground has thawed. Ice on the ponds is breaking up or gone. Skunk cabbage is up in the wet woods. The blackbirds have arrived from the South and are noisy in the trees. Already my early bulbs are in bloom—the species crocuses in February, the bigger ones in March, along with scilla and the first daffodils. My witch hazel has been in fragrant yellow bloom for a month. It is forty-five degrees and I lie happily in the mud, poking seeds in. Spring has come for me.

So I am ready to celebrate it in the seder even when the holiday comes in March, although in New England, that can feel perverse. I remember a Pesach with my old commune in Cambridge, Massachusetts. We were to bring the main dish and the tzimmes, when a sudden snowstorm trapped us in our houses. Ira and I ended up eating the meal for ten ourselves and holding our own seder for two. The wind rattled the windows and piled up drifts against the doors. While we were reading the haggadah, the lights went out and we had to continue by the light of the Pesach candles.

A connection to nature underlies Jewish holidays. All feasts and commemorations that preceded and helped to enrich Pesach were recognitions of the season—lambing time, the earliest harvest of grain, the time of birth and rebirth. Our haggadah always has some little ode to spring, either mine or an excerpt from the Song of Songs immediately preceding the blessing for the Karpas. The Song of Songs is traditionally associated with Pesach because of Pesach's origins as a festival of spring, the season of

lambing, of arranging marriages in those nomadic days that preceded Egypt, the season when the earth gives up its first foods.
You might select some passage to read. Marcia Falk's translation
is beautiful. You might also read a passage over the Charoset, if
you like.

Karpas

I am one of those weird people
who eat the parsley garnish
off restaurant dinners, not
only mine but yours and his.
I will nibble them all.

I like the sharp almost
gritty bite of the leaves,
its formidable green,
its prickly rank scent,
its persistence under snow.

Dip the leaves curly
as pubic hairs into the tears
in the bowl, remembering
old pain and the strength
to endure and grow on.

An herb whose white root
grows down and down into the earth,

so that gardeners say it goes
to the devil twice
before it stretches up,

slow to germinate, slow growing
and then weedy and stubborn,
surviving drought, neglect,
frost, the iron weight of winter.
Its leaves dipped in salt water

is the taste of spring—not
the sentimental spring of bunnies
and florists' bouquets, but real
season of hungry deer and geese
honking tiny in the gray sky,

of dirt thawing with the bones
of winter exposed to the sun,
old deaths and the cost
of survival, the miracle
of days growing longer like hair.

We dip the organic into the inorganic. We dip green into white salt, as if remembering winter as we say good-bye to it. We dip the easily bruised and wilted into that which does not oxidize or decay. So many meanings swirl around us as we dip the parsley into the salt water and eat it. Find the ones that speak to you. If you try to do that with every bit of the seder, you'll experience your own real Pesach.

7
The Four Questions

*T*he seder, when it works, creates a night of questions. We question the elements in the ritual, wrestling with each of them like Jacob with the angel to force out for ourselves a meaning that works for each of us individually and perhaps may work for us as a group, a community. We question ourselves, our relationship to history, our relationship to our fellow human beings, our relationship to our own values. How are we living out our values or failing to? What holds us back, within or without? What is our Egypt and the Egypt of the time and place in which we find ourselves? What must we do to liberate ourselves? What must we do to liberate others? The seder should not be a ritual conducted by a leader over the heads of those seated around the seder table, but one in which everyone present participates and has a hand in creating.

The Four Questions are part of the exploration of the meaning of the Exodus and its accompanying remembrances and rituals. If we are each to feel as if we personally took part, work is needed. We are required to put in some emotional effort, to empathize with those who suffered then and who have suffered since then and who suffer now through oppression of many kinds. We are required to take part in some intellectual labor, in ferreting out, re-creating or creating anew every part of the ritual and the telling.

The Four Questions are designed to involve children. One of the commandments of Pesach is to tell your child or children about the Exodus and Pesach, their history and meanings. It is a commandment to make sure that your children feel they are part of the Jewish people. Still, the Four Questions is one of the parts of the ritual that you may want to do in Hebrew before you do it in English. This means more work. The youngest child, in advance, should practice the Hebrew and learn the meaning. It is not necessary that a five-year-old learn to read the Hebrew alphabet. Use a transliteration and the melody. Melodies help us memorize. Most people who say they cannot memorize a poem or material for a test can remember the lyrics of a hundred songs without even trying.

That means some quality time with the kid or kids who will do the Four Questions, persuading, explaining, practicing, making clear what is going to happen at the seder. If the kid enjoys showing off, that's great. It's show-off time. Of course, sometimes the Four Questions are asked by a thirty-two-year-old, who is the youngest person present. Well, that person should still practice so it goes smoothly. If the youngest is a baby, take the next youngest. I have witnessed a toddler being tortured to remember what meant nothing to the little boy until he ended up having a tantrum. That is not a good mood for a seder. The youngest should mean the youngest who can actually perform and is willing to do so.

Sometimes it is sad for an eight-year-old who really enjoyed mastering the Hebrew and the melody of the Four Questions to be replaced by a six-year-old the next year. Give the eight-year-old something special to do. Well ahead of the date, give him or her some songs to memorize or a particular part of the seder to study. Ask the eight-year-old to bring questions for discussion. Give a task so that this child does not feel replaced but rather that they have moved up a rank and are getting a more adult role. Peace in our time and our families, shalom. It is the custom in some families for every child to ask one of the questions. In Sephardic usage, the whole ensemble—everybody at the table—asks the questions in unison. Pick the model that works best for your family.

You can also split up the Hebrew and the English and have the youngest say the English and the next oldest, the Hebrew. At our seder, after the child recites the Four Questions, we usually have the parents or stepparents of the child answer them. Or we divide the answers between the parents and older siblings or anyone else having a close relationship to that child or children. Some people have the leader answer the questions. I prefer to move the leadership around.

But to return to the value of questioning: Judaism has always encouraged questions. Arguing and interpreting are part our tradition, to the degree that the besetting sin of halachic Judaism was *pilpul*, the ever finer points of argument for argument's sake. The Four Questions show us what we are supposed to be doing: questioning the meaning and purpose of the seder as a whole as well as individual parts. How is this night different from all other nights? There are as many answers to that question as there are individuals at every seder every year since Pesach was instituted. If we do not teach our children the meaning of the central rituals of being Jewish and if we do not find meaning ourselves in these rituals and activities, how shall we continue to be Jews? If we have to change the rituals and the activities in order to make them part of our lives, a part we cherish and can pass along to others, then we change in order to survive. The book of Exodus commands us only to observe the Paschal sacrifice, eat matzoh and bitter herbs, and tell our children about being slaves and then becoming

free. It is our birth story as a people. After the destruction of the Second Temple, the rabbis found ways to carry out the Pesach commandment with no Temple and thus no sacrifice or no great public gathering.

For two thousand years we have celebrated Pesach in homes with our friends, our family, with strangers, and at others' seders when we have none of our own. The haggadah changed. Charoset was added. Karpas and Maror produced an offspring, Chazeret. The ritual with the middle matzoh and the afikomen was instituted. The idea of hiding the afikomen and then getting a reward, or alternatively, the children "stealing" it from the leader and then ransoming it for a prize, were added—to pique and keep the interest of the children. Certain psalms and prayers, blessings and songs became customary. Wine was incorporated into every section of the haggadah. The Talmud presents other possibilities of questions. There's nothing fixed in stone with these four questions, although it is pleasant to sing the traditional melody.

The Four Questions have evolved over time. If you look at historical texts, you will find that originally there were only three questions, and the third was concerned with eating roasted meat. After the destruction of the Second Temple, there was no sacrifice and thus no Pashcal Lamb to share, so that question vanished. The question about eating bitter herbs was not there originally; it was added later.

You can replace any questions that don't make sense to you. The least useful part of the Four Questions is the one about reclining, at least for me. We cannot possibly cram more than sixteen people into our smallish dining room. To get sixteen in, we have to remove all the furniture except the extended fully leaved table, the chairs, and the china cabinet, which we cannot move without danger of breaking all our dishes. Nobody reclines. Anyone who has to use the bathroom displaces at least two or three other people in order to get out of his or her assigned seating. As the leader, I am the only one who can bounce out of my seat, stand up and sit down easily. Not only can no one recline, but everyone has to keep their elbows strictly to themselves. Every chair in the house is in use, and some years we have to borrow chairs.

So we replace the fourth question with one that we ask every year:

On all other nights when we dine together, we have plenty of room. Why tonight are we wedged in elbow to elbow?

The answer:

Because we want to share our seder with as many people as we can cram into this little room. To be together every year is precious beyond telling. And we are bidden in the haggadah to say, Let all who are hungry come and eat, and let all who are needy come and share with us. We are sure that those of you who have come a long way are hungry, and if you are here, you must be in need of a seder. Therefore, we welcome in as many people as we can cram into our space.

It is enlightening to engage with whatever haggadah you use. You want to know why you are doing each step. If you and your group cannot tease out any meaning, then either you are not trying hard enough or it is time to discard that piece of the ritual and replace it with something that still resonates in your lives now.

You might ask why there were originally four sons instead of four children. Why were the girls not allowed to question or to take part? Why have women been excluded from an active role in Judaism? Why are the leaders of Jewish community groups to this day largely or exclusively men? Why do so many people think of the Eternal One as male? How can we change this to include all of our experiences and voices?

You might want to find a question that applies to a present situation, such as: Why are we at war when none of the excuses for war make sense? Or why, if we are the best off country in the world, are so many homeless and so many hungry? Why do some need food stamps and handouts from charity pantries when they work long hours for minimum wage? Make your own questions.

Although Pesach commemorates the founding of our people as a nation and our flight into freedom, it's not the Fourth of July. It's closer to Martin Luther King's wishful cry, "Free at last." The seder reminds us of slavery, insists we explore its meaning and pain, insists we identify with those who are still enslaved. That section of the traditional answer also says that whoever elaborates and develops the story of Exodus deserves praise. To elaborate—decorate, explore, develop, re-create—the story is an act we are encouraged to carry out. So do it. Tell the story, when you come to it. Or, as an alternative, discuss the nature of slavery itself. Are there still slaves?

According to Web sites by antislavery groups, like Anti-Slavery International, there are between twenty and thirty million people in slavery today, more if you include children in forced labor. Some are chattel slaves, as the Israelites were. Some end up as slaves because of debt. Others sign a contract for a job and end up in another country working in sweatshops for barely enough to survive. Women are forced into brothels as sexual slaves. Children are sold to pay their parents' debts or because the parents mistakenly believe their children will be better off. Children are kidnapped and forced into sexual slavery. There are a few groups fighting slavery, including some who buy slaves to set them free, but most people now are ignorant of the extent of slavery or prefer not to know about it.

In some Sephardic traditions (not Spanish or Portuguese), after the Four Questions the leader leaves the room and returns with the afikomen wrapped in a bag or napkin over his or her shoulder. Some simply send the reader around the table with the afikomen. More questioning follows, for instance:

"Who are you?"

"I am a Jew."

"Where are you from?"

"Egypt."

"What did you do there?"

"I was a slave."

"How long did you travel to arrive here?"

"For forty years."

"Why?"

"To be free."

In some Mizraki customs, a child actually goes out of the house, or just out of the room, and knocks on the door, then is questioned as above. For some, it is a custom for everybody to trek around the table as if on an Exodus journey. It's not a bad idea to try out some form of this, particularly if there are children, for it wakes them up. Do not be afraid to vary the questions in English, to knock out any that have lost their relevance and replace them with other questions that you feel will stir up the participants and make them truly interact with the haggadah.

8
The Four Children

𝒜fter the Four Questions comes the description of the four children who ask or do not ask questions about what is going on. Why do we have a seder at all? Why isn't this like any other company meal? Why is there all this mumbo jumbo? All this stuff you're talking about happened so long ago; who cares? What's all this Hebrew? Why can't I leave the table and watch TV? But at the same time, the four children also describe attitudes that adults bring to the seder. There's something a bit judgmental in this description of attitudes, a turn away from the willingness to encourage all kinds of questioning. We'll try to change that.

The seder represents a perfect time for educating children and adults together about Judaism and Jewish history and practice. It's a whole evening of reading, talking, arguing, explaining, and singing followed by lots of eating, then reading, talking, arguing, explaining, and singing some more. That's one reason it is so vital not to allow the seder to be a drag. Don't bore the kids. Don't turn it into Moses on Ice or Exodus Disney-style, but get involved with the ritual to make it more engaging. Give the children memories of being Jewish in a context that will strengthen their identity and give them warmth and pride, mixed with the development of compassion. Few of the children who attend our seder have had formal religious training. Some come from intermarried families. A couple of those in attendance have been bar or bat mitzvahed, but otherwise there is little Judaism in their lives. Therefore we have an added responsibility to make the seder special. It may be the most meaningful contact with Judaism in their young lives.

A seder is a wonderful opportunity to get everyone at the table talking about political and historical events. It's a good time to get each person thinking about his or her own place in history and in society and the world in its largest sense. Don't hesitate to bring in your own family's history—maybe your grandparents made an exodus from the Pale of Settlement in Russia or from a shtetl in Lithuania. Maybe your parents made an exodus from Algeria or Syria straight here or via Israel. Maybe people in your family fled the Holocaust to America. Maybe survivors in your family managed to overcome great obstacles to reach Israel or Canada or the United States. Make the connections.

Maybe there are refugees from troubles in Africa or the Middle East or Europe in your village or town or city. Do whatever you can to make the notion of fleeing Egypt real by drawing contemporary parallels. Many people have uprooted themselves to get away from disaster and oppression, to remove themselves from slavery and danger. If you have invited people with a different heritage to your seder, they may have family histories that can relate to the notion of exodus.

The Wise Child is the first one mentioned, the child who can ask in a way that reveals that this child already has some religious education and understands that there are laws and customs that produce the ritual everyone is experiencing. What are the commandments and laws that bear upon us, this group, this community of which I am a member? This child is aware of being a Jew and simply wants the education to proceed and the details to be revealed. Go to the head of the class! Of course later on, this child may be a nuisance, commenting on the right way to do everything, the way that person's family or synagogue did it. But for now, Wise Child is on the right track. (I was a Wise Child type at my grandma's seders. Fortunately the only boy among her grandchildren lived way out in Everett, Washington, and thus offered no competition.) The Wise Child may become arrogant, we should remember, and turn into the Jew who is always telling everybody else how much he or she knows. We're trying to get rid of the leaven of pride tonight, and the Wise Child could easily puff up with pride.

Then comes the Wicked Child, who is fed up with all the fuss. Perhaps the child has been told, "No, you can't watch the TV in the family room and you can't take your supper in there." The child is finding the seder a bother and asks, probably pouting, "Why do you do all this every year?" by implication announcing, "It means nothing to me." The problem is not so much in failing to understand Pesach, for it is our duty to make her or him understand what is going on and to conduct it in such a way that the process is engaging. The problem here is "you." This child is already separating him- or herself from the community. "You guys can do what you want; I would rather do my own thing." Judaism is a communal activity. We have to coax this child, persuade this child back into the community. The traditional haggadah says to set the child's teeth on edge. Maybe they had in mind a good knock upside the head, but parents are not encouraged along those lines nowadays. The traditional haggadah suggests that if you aren't in the community, you don't join the Exodus. You would remain enslaved. If you believe that history has nothing to teach you, you will learn nothing from history. But history has a way of coming to get us. To forget history is to make ourselves stupid and naive. We should also remember that many children's experience of Judaism is so dry and so heavy with uncomprehended ritual that the "wicked" may only be expressing an honest alienation that we must try to overcome, not by insisting but by demonstrating the richness of what we offer.

The third child is the Simple Child, who does not know how to ask the right or insightful questions. Many times we all behave this way. Something goes by us and we don't want to make fools of ourselves by asking about it. We are afraid to ask directions in the street or on the road. We don't want to admit that we have no idea what people are talking about. Therefore we fake it. We pretend to have seen a particular movie or read a book people are talking about. Or we just stare at the walls, have more to eat or drink, and start zoning out.

The Simple Child or the Simple Child in us has to be led to ask questions, has to feel from others' reactions that ignorance is only a sin if you dwell in it comfortably. If you are willing to learn, other people will open up. People often enjoy teaching something that they know about. If you let them teach you, soon you will know too. We can encourage questions, so long as they are real ones. Some people ask questions to put others down or to make others feel foolish. That is an attack, not a desire for knowledge. The Simple Child would probably like to understand but hasn't a clue where to start. So make a starting point. In a way, visitors to our community have the same problem, sometimes not knowing where to begin questioning what they experience or see.

Then comes the child too young to ask or understand. Just give that child reassurance that this is a good event as well as an important event in this home, this house, this community. Make this child feel, You are a part of all this, and it is good.

Then there is a Fifth Child that some of us include. We say:

On this night we remember too a Fifth Child. This is a child of the Shoah who did not survive to ask. In silence we remember that child's forced silence. In silence we remember that dark time. In silence we remember Passovers Jews spent in the partisan forests, in the ghettos, in the camps, at forced labor in the factories until they were worked to death; we remember that Pesach night when the Warsaw ghetto rose in revolt. The Fifth Child is of that generation never allowed to grow up and join the community.

I have also seen the Fifth Child described as the Jew who has dropped out, perhaps converted, perhaps just overassimilated and unwilling to bother, the grown-up child who says, "This just isn't for me. It's a lot of anachronistic nonsense."

Perhaps you may find in the four children some tendency of your own or your guests. For instance, when you are faced with something puzzling or something you think is way outside your own experience, how do you react? Do you ask a great many specific questions aimed at increasing your comprehension so that you are no longer confused? If you do know something about the subject, do you show off that knowledge? Do you simply wave the unknown subject away, perhaps making a joke of it? Are you convinced that what you don't understand can't hurt you and is not worth your effort? Are you contemptuous of those who bother to study and learn? Do you simply pretend to know already and let it go by, not wanting to expose your ignorance? Are you too embarrassed by what you don't already comprehend to ask about it? Do you simply have no idea where to begin and hope that there will be time, some time, some future distant time, in which you will learn all about this thing that is opaque to you?

There is another way to look at the Four Children—they are aspects of ourselves in our confrontation with the strange, the threatening, the mysterious, the knowledge that requires effort and work to encompass. Probably at different times and in different situations of our lives, we have each been all of these children. Some parents may bristle at children being singled out to be labeled. If so, call these characters the Wise Guy, the Arrogant Guy, and so forth. It's your seder. Make it work for you.

9
Maggid: The Telling

One of the basic commandments of Pesach is the telling of the Exodus from Egypt. In the traditional haggadah the story is told briefly, then more fully but always obliquely, mostly with an emphasis on Hashem leading the people to freedom. You have to choose how much detail you want to include and how you want to tell the story. Maybe as in the traditional approach, you want to emphasize the role of a higher power. Maybe you are not comfortable with that, don't really believe it when you are honest with yourself, and want a story about people, including Moses, Aaron, and Miriam. Whatever emphasis you put on various aspects of the story and who the movers and shakers are, be sure you believe what you are saying. How can you move your children if you aren't telling them what you really think? If your belief is more traditional, share it. If you think the story is just that, tell it as a stirring story. Get into the characters. If you see it as a parable about liberation, go with that.

Some families act out the story. Others tell it dramatically. If you have children, you might want to involve them in creating a playlet, taking parts, perhaps making and wearing costumes. You are commanded to tell the story of the Exodus, but any which way you want to or can imagine, try! Everybody is convinced they know the story, giving way to snooze time at the table, so you want to try to wake people up and get them to encounter the story freshly. Camcorder a play. Use puppets. Have the children make drawings or a long mural on a roll of paper depicting the primary events. Role-play—which works with adults and stimulates them as well as it does children. Each person becomes a character in the story—a slave girl, a brick maker, a mother whose baby boy was killed—and speaks a paragraph or two in the first person. You must give them each a character to become and a concrete situation so that they have a place to begin to imagine who they are and what they would be feeling.

The Maggid opens with *Ha lachma anya. . . .* "This is the bread of pain our ancestors ate in Egypt when they were slaves." The leader or the person reading at that moment points to the matzoh, which the leader uncovers. We are going to eat the same thin poor bread that they ate. Here we also welcome any who are hungry or in need—in need of a seder as well as in need of food or help or money or company.

When you list the Ten Plagues, shaking a drop of red wine onto the plate with the name of every plague is customary and meaningful. In our seder and many others, we say first the Hebrew word for the particular plague (like *kinim*), then the translation (*lice*), and then a modern plague—say, poverty or war or racism, whatever feels roughly equivalent. Sometimes when we have named the ten traditional plagues and those we have linked as modern plagues, I ask the participants to name other contemporary plagues. People cry out the plagues they want to acknowledge. Here's an example:

Let us recite the *Ten Plagues of Egypt*, then *Ten Plagues of our own time.*
As we read each ancient and modern plague, we dip a finger in our wine
and cast a single drop on our plate. This, our sages said, reminds us that
our happiness cannot be complete during our Festival of Freedom when
people remain enslaved. So with each plague, we take a little of our wine—
the beverage of joy—and cast it down. (Remember to pass the wine
around just before this, so that everyone has some wine to cast down. After
all, we have already drunk the first cup and not yet poured the second.)

THE TEN PLAGUES
(THROW A DROP ON THE PLATE WITH EACH)

DAM	BLOOD	POVERTY
TZFARDE'AH	FROGS	FROGLESSNESS: POISONING OUR ENVIRONMENT
KINIM	LICE	DISEASE
AROV	WILD BEASTS	GREED AND EXPLOITATION
DEVER	PESTILENCE	AIDS
SHKHERN	BOILS	CANCER
BARAD	HAIL	SEXISM
ARBEH	LOCUSTS	HUNGER
CHOSHECH	DARKNESS	RACISM
MAKAT BICHOROT	KILLING OF THE FIRSTBORN	GENOCIDE

Are there more plagues that consume us and threaten the earth? The leader can ask that question of the group and let everyone call out the names of what they consider plagues. Encourage any children present to call out what they considering threatening. Or perhaps we might want to pause and discuss if we ourselves are the worst plague upon the earth, if we are not destroying it and doing so rather quickly.

We are not encouraged to rejoice in the plagues, especially the last one, the death of so many firstborn, or to rejoice in the destruction of Pharaoh's army in the Sea of Reeds. The traditional haggadah tells us that when Egyptian soldiers and charioteers were drowning in the Sea of Reeds, the angels began to sing. Hashem silenced them, saying, "How can you sing while my children are dying?" The haggadah again reminds us that while we Jews have our Exodus and our Pesach, many other people suffer and must escape from and fight their oppression too.

What was slavery? What is a slave? What sets a slave apart from other people who work? What does a slave own? What choices has a slave? We need to explore the meaning of slavery before we proceed. Does the slave always revolt? If not, why not? What happens if a slave internalizes his or her master's values? If he or she accepts the master's opinion of the slave's worth? What does it mean to "internalize" oppression?

One of the reasons we tell the story is because the past is part of the present. "Those who cannot remember the past are condemned to repeat it," George Santayana wrote. G. K. Chesterton wrote, "The disadvantage of men not knowing the past is that they do not know the present." We will be enslaved again and again if we are not vigilant. If we do not protect our freedom, we will lose it. If we do not fight what limits and oppresses us, we will remain in chains. If we are not equally vigilant, we may enslave others. We are urged with every festival of the Jewish year to reenact parts of the past so that we not only remember them but also in some small way experience them. We are to live through the escape from slavery as if we were there, as best we can. We are to name and examine our own enslavements, inner and outer. What enslaves you? An addiction, a habit, a relationship, the past you won't let go of, envy, jealousy, material possessions? Pride of place? Shame?

Although it is not necessary to do this aloud, some participants will go through this self-examination willingly; others will strongly resist. They feel it as too intrusive or touchy-feely or liberal. I have had guests who groused through the whole haggadah; once we had a teenager who wore a propeller beanie and smirked at the proceedings. But as a leader, you have to try to get people to engage, even if you will sometimes, inevitably, fail with a few of those at the table. Try not to let one grouchy or unwilling guest spoil the evening for everybody else. Some people do come just to eat.

One year we followed a practice recommended by Rabbi Allen Ullman, with whom I have studied Torah on many occasions. We put pans of water on the floor—large baking pans with sides—and after we removed our shoes and socks, we all crossed the Sea of Reeds, imagining ourselves fleeing and asking ourselves what we are fleeing from and what we are going toward. Afterward, we had to mop up the floor because water splashed everywhere, creating a mess. This is nice symbolism and playacting but impractical in modern houses. If you live in a place where it is mild or warm at Pesach, consider taking everybody outside to cross the Sea of Reeds. It sure does wake people up, and outside it won't get all over the floor. Elementary as this exercise may sound, it jars complacency. It's the opposite of sitting around all dressed up, making chitchat, returning home stuffed but otherwise unchanged.

We struggle with the ancient story to wrestle out meaning for ourselves. It's not all that easy. We make parallels to the plagues, but the idea of the Eternal bringing down terrible troubles and destruction upon a whole people because of their ruler and their ruling class is a little hard for us to swallow now, even though we may behave the same way in our own invasions of other countries. It is worthwhile to bring up these issues and struggle with them together. What is beautiful and moving in the story to me is the assertion of the right to freedom of every human being. No one is unimportant because of how little they possess—in the case of slaves, they do not even possess themselves—or how poor they are. Every human being has the right to be free, and when people are oppressed economically, physically, by being taught they are less—as women have been in most of recorded history—then they can and must struggle for their freedom and we should help. We think of people fleeing into the desert with hastily baked bread and a few rags on their backs. What does that bring to mind? Who flees today? From what? Into what? We might consider the plight of the homeless; refugees penned in camps; political fugitives; fugitives from oppression and poverty; millions displaced by war, their lives and families obliterated. We might think of people forced from their homes by hurricanes, fires, tsunamis, volcanic eruptions.

Or if it is easier for us to empathize, let us consider an Exodus of one, or one with her children and sometimes a companion animal: the woman who is leaving abuse in fear of her life and who, in spite of years of torment and abasement, decides she has had enough or that she wants something different for her children, and so flees, often with nothing more than the clothes on her back.

The Exodus story also anchors us to our lives rather than to an afterlife. The slaves don't die and go to heaven and find reward for their misery. They get up and go. They leave slavery and flee into the desert together. Jews are historical beings. We began at a certain time and place and we are enjoined to create our many Exodus activities where we are and when we are. Here and now. Tonight. Our duty is to make the Exodus real and meaningful by understanding slavery and freedom and exploring their meaning to us.

That is the real mitzvah of the Maggid—to reanimate an ancient story. The traditional haggadah tells of Rabbi Akiva and four other rabbis staying up all night at their seder. I had always been told that this story was to demonstrate an ideal seder with discussion of every point. It is only in recent years that I learned that what Rabbi Akiva was probably doing was plotting a revolt against Roman occupation, planning to take part in Bar Kochba's uprising. That was their Egypt and their attempted Exodus.

We have had many flights and relocations during our long and often bloody history. Hence this poem, which we include at this point in our seder:

Maggid

The courage to let go of the door, the handle.
The courage to shed the familiar walls whose very
stains and leaks are comfortable as the little moles
of the upper arm; stains that recall a feast,
a child's naughtiness, a loud blattering storm
that slapped the roof hard, pouring through.

The courage to abandon the graves dug into the hill,
the small bones of children and the brittle bones
of the old whose marrow hunger had stolen;
the courage to desert the tree planted and only
begun to bear; the riverside where promises were
shaped; the street where their empty pots were broken.

The courage to leave the place whose language you learned
as early as your own, whose customs however dangerous or demeaning, bind you like a halter
you have learned to pull inside, to move your load;
the land fertile with the blood spilled on it;
the roads mapped and annotated for survival.

The courage to walk out of the pain that is known
into the pain that cannot be imagined,
mapless, walking into the wilderness, going
barefoot with a canteen into the desert;
stuffed in the stinking hold of a rotting ship
sailing off the map into dragon's mouths,

Cathay, India, Siberia, goldeneh medinah,
leaving bodies by the way like abandoned treasure.
So they walked out of Egypt. So they bribed their way
out of Russia under loads of straw; so they steamed
out of the bloody smoking charnel house of Europe
on overloaded freighters forbidden all ports—

out of pain into death or freedom or a different
painful dignity, into squalor and politics.
We Jews are all born wanderers, with shoes
under our pillows and a memory of blood that is ours
raining down. We honor only those Jews who changed
tonight, those who chose the desert over bondage

who walked into the strange and became strangers
and gave birth to children who could look down
on them, standing on their shoulders, for having
been slaves. We honor those who let go of every-
thing but freedom, who ran, who revolted, who fought,
who became other by saving themselves.

We use this poem in my haggadah just before the Dayenu. It
connects the Exodus with other traumatic events, other diaspo-
ras, other migrations in Jewish history. The word strangers is
repeated again and again in Torah. Why? Why are we reminded
of our duty to strangers, not to oppress them, to treat them
kindly? Have we not often throughout history been strangers?
Don't we sometimes, even in the country we inhabit, even if we

were born in the United States and lived here all our lives, feel like strangers in the overwhelming culture based on Christianity?

When I was in grade school, all the students sang Christmas and Easter songs. I had to learn the words and sing these songs. I particularly hated the Easter songs. To this day, I bristle at Christmas carols, for it reminds me of my anomalous position in school. There were only two Jews in my grade school, and the other was African-American. We were put on hall guard duty together always, because being Jews was more important than race in the eyes of the authorities. We were strangers together.

Sometimes in the hyperreligious Jesus Saves parts of the country, I feel very much a stranger and sometimes an unwelcome one. We Jews have often been the strangers—the ones who don't celebrate Christmas and Easter, the ones who may not eat the same foods or who shun some of the foods others enjoy, the ones who have different holidays with odd names. In a society where some leaders proclaim it as a Christian society and want to incorporate Christianity into public rituals and into laws and public education, we may well feel like strangers.

After the Maggid, it is traditional and great fun to sing "Dayenu." We like to bang on the table in the chorus. We sing it loudly, if not well.

However, right before it, since we are considering on this night what liberation means, we often say a piece that recognizes how far we have to go in *tikkun olam*, repair of our world—our unending task. The pattern that you may fill with your own content goes: If we do this, but we neglect that, it is not enough, reciting a litany of projects to repair the world and bring justice and peace. Here are some examples of what I mean. We do this just before the Dayenu, but I know other people do something similar right after it.

Dayenu

Once we were slaves in the land of Egypt. Let that memory of that time teach us to value freedom for everyone. Dayenu.

BUT if we cherish freedom, yet forget political prisoners and those unjustly imprisoned here and abroad, it will not be enough . . .

AND if we work for those unjustly imprisoned, but ignore those who are denied their full opportunities and respect by racism, it will not be enough . . .

If we work toward a world where civil rights belong to all, but hunger remains, it will not be enough . . .

AND if we dream of a peaceful and well-fed world, but ignore the fate of those who must live in violence and in danger, it will not be enough . . .

AND if we demand freedom and peace, but we neglect women's struggles for safety and dignity, it will not be enough . . .

AND if we struggle for the rights of women everywhere, but we are callous to the rights of other living beings with whom we share the land and the sea, it will not be enough . . .

If we cherish the environment here but permit our government to export destruction and pollution abroad, it will not be enough . . .

If we work to prevent exploitation and sweatshops in underdeveloped countries, but neglect to preserve the State of Israel, it will not be enough . . .

AND if we cherish the State of Israel, but we neglect our responsibility to help create a safe and peaceful Palestinian homeland, it will not be enough . . .

FOR if we talk about ending domination and despair, but we fail to act on our beliefs, it will not be enough. In truth, it will only be enough when we have put an end to human misery and suffering. As Rabbi Tarfon said, "It is not your obligation to complete the task but neither are you free to desist from it" (Pirkei Avot, Sayings of the Fathers).

And none of it matters if we invade other nations on faked excuses to gain power and riches and we bring down terror and death on others, as we do not wish to be done to us.

But if we do not give up but try always to change what needs changing and fix what needs fixing, as much as is in our power and ability, then it is enough. Dayenu.

Each person has their own Dayenu of gratitude for what they have been able to do that might well have been denied them. "If I get this better job but do not spend more time with my family, then I have not improved our lives." "If I spend more time with my children, but do not teach them about the lives of other children." "If I teach them about poverty and oppression, but don't try to do something about it." You get the idea. There are many ways to deal with this section of the seder, before or after you sing the song. You have to sing the song, in any event, as it is too much fun to omit. Again it wakes everyone up. In Mizraki usage, it is customary for each person to gently whip the person next to him or her with onions, leeks, or stalks of celery to recall the slaves' beating by their masters. That should also work to keep things lively. I have seen many versions of the Dayenu that deal with "what is not sufficient" and urge you to create your own.

10
Z'roah: The Lamb Shank

Z'roah, the lamb shank, is one of the mutable parts of the seder plate objects. Some people use a chicken wing. But even if I don't serve lamb as the main dish of the meal, I like to stay with the symbolism of the lamb shank and its associations with sacrifice and the smear of blood on the doors of those who intended to resist and leave. Vegetarians I know have used everything from a potato to a yam. A beet is sometimes chosen, because it is red. Another replacement is a piece of tofu shaped like a bone.

I buy a lamb shank well in advance, because it seems as if butchers, unless they are kosher (and there are no kosher butchers within fifty miles of where I live), always seem to be astonished that suddenly lamb shanks are highly desirable. They run out. As a matter of fact, I cook with lamb shanks not infrequently during the year. I like them because they give a lot of flavor if cooked slowly. Without eating a lot of meat, you can have a whole dish that is delicious. Part of our family tradition is that in the week before Pesach, I cook the lamb shanks in a casserole or other dish and then I keep one for the seder plate; two if we are going out to a second seder. A bit of meat should be left clinging to the bone.

Here's a recipe for lamb shanks if you would like to follow that practice.

◎

Braised Lamb Shanks with White Beans

1 tablespoon olive oil
1 lamb shank per person
1 onion, diced
1 celery stalk, diced
2 large carrots, diced
6 cloves garlic, minced
1 can cannellini beans—this is a good amount for 2 or 3
1 cup dry red wine (I often use wine left over from
    other meals.)
½ cup chicken broth
1 jar tomatoes
Some tomato sauce
1 teaspoon chopped fresh thyme or ½ teaspoon
    dried thyme
1 bay leaf
Salt and freshly ground pepper to taste
1 tablespoon grated lemon zest
Juice of 1 lemon
2 tablespoons chopped fresh parsley

If you are cooking for more than three, you want to increase amounts according to the number of people.

On medium high heat, warm the olive oil. Brown the lamb shanks on all sides, 10 to 12 minutes. Take them out, turn down the flame, and add the onion, celery, and carrots to the pan and sauté 8 to 10 minutes, till tender. Add the garlic and cook, stirring, for 2 minutes.

Add beans, wine, broth, tomatoes, tomato sauce, thyme, bay leaf, and salt and pepper. Stir to mix. Add the lamb shanks, bring to a simmer, and reduce heat to low. Cover and simmer until the beans are tender and the meat is nearly falling off the bone, 2½ to 3 hours. If you keep the heat low or put it in a medium oven—325°F or so— you can go off and do something else. It's not a fussy dish. You put it on and, as long as you don't have the heat too high, it will take care of itself.

Five minutes before you're ready to eat, add lemon zest, lemon juice, and parsley. Serve immediately. You can use bread to sop up the sauce.

◎

If you would prefer a simpler recipe, here's one.

Simply place a lamb shank for each person in a baking dish with a lid. Turn the oven to 350°F or, if you are doing very slow cooking because you're going out or off to do something else, 325°F or even 300°F.

Cut up an onion and some garlic. Add some of these: cut-up smallish potatoes, carrots, celery, winter squash. Then add herbs like parsley, mint, thyme, or savory. Then add red wine halfway up in the pan. Add salt and, if you like, a little sweet spiciness, such as cinnamon or allspice.

Then just put it in the oven and go away. Come back about 30 minutes before serving and add green beans— about ½ pound for two.

It's a one-dish supper and a great use of lamb shanks.

You can also cook the lamb shanks with red wine, onions, garlic, allspice, mint, and basil (carrots are optional) for 1 ½ hours. Then add green beans and lemon juice and cook for another 20 to 30 minutes. A wonderful one-dish supper, good with bread or rice that can also be made with other vegetables: zucchini or kale, for instance.

From any of these dishes, you just save a bone with a little meat still on it, stick it in a plastic bag in the freezer, and you have your lamb shank ready for Pesach.

Okay, we have the lamb shank. Now why is it on the plate to begin with?

Lamb Shank—Z'roah Pesach

It grosses out many of my friends.
They don't eat meat, let alone
place it on a ritual platter.
I am not so particular, or more so.

Made of flesh and bone, liver
and sinew, salty blood and brain,
I know they weren't ghosts who trekked
out of baked mud huts into the desert.

Blood was spilled, red and real:
first ours, then theirs. Blood
splashed on the doorposts proclaimed
in danger the rebellion within.

We are pack and herd animals.
One Jew is not a Jew, but we are
a people together, plural, joined.
We were made flesh and we bled.

And we fled, under the sign
of the slaughtered lamb to live
and die for each other. We are
meat that thinks and sings.

Why a lamb? Well, they are probably the oldest domesticated herd animal, along with goats. Sheep were precious to our ancestors, for they provide meat, milk, and wool. You can clothe yourself in them, eat yogurt or cheese made from ewe's milk, and then eat the whole animal. They have been bred over the millennia—and I do mean millennia—to be stupider, smaller, more docile, and with less dangerous horns, if any. Archaeologists place the domestication of sheep from southern Turkey to southern Iran, in the Taurus and Zagreb Mountains. They date evidence of sheep domestication back to eight or nine thousand years ago, although apparently at that age, it's difficult to separate sheep and goat bones. We seem always to have aimed at making animals we were going to keep around less aggressive (except for roosters) and sometimes smaller. Consider that the cow was somehow bred from the Auroch, which was fierce, quite powerful, weighed three tons, and stood seven feet high. You get the idea, although you have to wonder how our ancestors ever did.

Sheep and goats were the preferred sacrificial animals in the Middle East, although cattle were also sacrificed. In Judaism, Christianity, and Islam there was (and is for Islam) actual or symbolic sacrifice of a lamb or sheep. You probably remember that when Abraham was about to sacrifice his son Isaac, he was commanded to kill instead a wild ram caught in a thicket—and indeed, this must have appeared a great improvement to most folks. Baal demands your babies; Hashem just wants a sheep. Lambs, if you have ever watched them, seem the picture of innocent enjoyment, so perhaps they are perceived as a being free from blemish or fault to be offered up. Rams were powerful, an embodiment of male energy.

Sheep are luckier than cows in the modern world, since they

are usually put to pasture rather than confined in stalls. They wander eating grass, stubble, shrubs under the watchful eyes of a dog, a llama (preferred in New England because they can success-fully fight our coyotes, which are 60 percent wolf here), or a sheep-herder. They were readily moved about by nomadic people and are still often herded from pasture to pasture, perhaps up on the mountains in spring and down to the lowlands in fall. We con-tinue to prize sheep's milk cheeses like Roquefort, pecorino, Romano, and feta. I have had it as milk in a village in Greece, but I think most Westerners would rather consume it as cheese—and it's far more profitable that way.

People have always prized meat, however little of it they got via hunting and later by animal husbandry. Feasts are generally occasions for eating meat (or if you're in a region where the fatti-est, most delicious protein is salmon, then it's salmon at your pot-latch). When people see their gods as bigger and more powerful but in a body similar to their own, they figure the gods would like some meat, too—and that way maybe they won't get jealous and might help out the next time when hunting or raising ani-mals. We can't get away from noticing that sacrificing an animal, even if it's done by the priest in the Temple, is a fairly primitive activity—even though it was a fine public occasion and every-body ate the sacrifice. Presumably, of course, the smoke and odor were sufficient for the Higher Power. Some authorities say that the sacrifice of a perfect lamb or kid was a replacement for the sacrifice of a firstborn or other child—as there are echoes of such sacrifice in Torah with Isaac and with Jephthah's daughter. Priests of Baal did sacrifice babies still in the time after the Exodus and simultaneously with the development of Judaism up through the destruction of the First Temple. Today, however you look at it, the notion that The Eternal requests a dead animal burnt seems a bit hard to stomach. This is one of those contradictions and weirdnesses we usually do not talk about.

There is for many people a prickle of embarrassment at that bone lying on the seder plate, a reminder that we are animals who eat other animals. Describing it as the outstretched arm of Hashem leading the Israelites out of Egypt doesn't help much. It doesn't look like an outstretched arm, and for most of us, any notion we may have of the Eternal has neither arms nor legs and certainly does not reside in a bit of cooked bone with some meat still attached.

What do we make of this? I have tried to take this on in the poem above, but I will consider it again. The lamb was the traditional sacrifice in Temple days, and it was eaten as part of the ceremony of Pesach. The instructions to Moses before the Exodus are for each household to cook a young unblemished lamb (or goat—but that somehow disappeared from our tradition; many cultures still eat goats with relish—in the Caribbean and in Italy, for instance) and roast it. Its blood is to be smeared on the doorposts and lintels of each house of those who intended to follow Moses out of Egypt. Then those houses marked with blood would be spared the death of the firstborn.

There is no liberation without struggle and few achieved without violence. Freedom is, unfortunately, usually won with blood. So perhaps we should consider the little shank bone a reminder of the frequent cost of liberation in human society. And to remember that in war or revolt, animals die at least as often as people do; whole landscapes die. Unless you want to pretty up the notion of revolution or rebellion or people seeking their freedom, take a good look at the shank bone. In order to be free, people have to take chances and have to be willing to be injured or to die for their cause. Blood all too frequently is the price of freedom.

Passover gobbled up previous holidays that were amalgamated into it. One was the time when a pastoral people stopped moving around long enough for the ewes to give birth and the lambs to grow enough to be able to travel. In spring at a fixed time, they would gather in oases or fertile spots. It was a time to enjoy, to give thanks, to arrange marriages and make alliances. Presumably they danced and sang. Certainly they sacrificed a young lamb or goat to ensure fertility and abundance in the coming pastoral year. Later the sacrifice had to occur at the Temple, a thanksgiving ritual of a pastoral people whose wealth was counted in sheep, goats, in some places, cattle. Once again, the people gathered together to feast, worship, celebrate, and communicate.

The Festival of Matzoh was originally a celebration of the beginning of the first grain harvest of the year. Originally this month brought the new year. Exodus was such an overwhelming experience and story that it preempted the earlier festivals into itself, and they became one powerful occasion. So the original sacrifice of the lamb and the celebration of the first harvest of wheat or barley and perhaps a dedication of the firstborn to The Eternal fed into the story of redemption and escape into freedom.

I like the shank bone because it reminds me of the cost of freedom. I find it a humbling emblem of our human condition, what we do to survive. Besides, the cooking and eating of the lamb dish that provides the shank bones is a prelude to Pesach for me. It moves my mind toward the holiday and its meaning. Like dealing with chametz, preparing the shank bone begins the approach of Pesach with its renewal socially, religiously, personally.

Cats seem to have little interest in the shank bone, but I had a friend who had trouble. She had laid out the ritual objects on the seder plate and went to get dressed before her guests arrived. When she came back into the dining room, the bone was gone and some of the dishes had been knocked off the seder plate. Her dog had run off with the shank bone. She was uncertain what to do, since she didn't have another. She chased the dog and recovered the bone. She rinsed it off and put it back on the plate in its proper place—after all, no one was going to eat it—locked up her dog in the back of the house, and proceeded to get ready for the seder. So if you have a dog, remember that it may be Z'roah Pesach to you but it's just a fine bone to Fido. Beware of the dog. That's one advantage for vegetarians who replace the bone with tofu or a beet: at least you don't have to worry about the family pet carrying it off.

For the rest of us, the lamb bone is a precious reminder of the cost of freedom. We don't get free by wishing for it. Too often, the innocent pay along with the guilty.

Bread in any form has a particularly important, sacred, and symbolic place in Jewish life. Most of us don't bless our salads or tuna fish casseroles before we eat them, but we bless the challah on Shabbat before we consume it. Perhaps bread is special because originally it was the main thing that people had to eat after farming began—grain in some form, baked into cakes, boiled into dumplings, fried into pancakes, and baked into breads. People actually had begun harvesting lots of wild wheat and barley twenty-three thousand years ago, as evidenced by remains excavated by archaeologists near Lake Tiberias in Israel on a site with grinding stones in remnants of huts. In the Taurus Mountains of southeastern Turkey, einkorn wheat—one of the so-called founder plants of agriculture—seems to have originated, for there is a wild wheat growing in that area to this day that is genetically similar enough to be an ancestor. It is now believed that einkorn wheat was domesticated in that region about ten thousand years ago.

Anybody who has ever kneaded bread and let it rise, slapped it down and kneaded it again, experiences bread as something living. It grows like a chicken or a puppy, but ever so much faster. With challah, if you are making it yourself, you are supposed to take off a small piece the size of an olive and to leave that in the oven to burn. This seems an ancient and perhaps pagan custom, to sacrifice a little piece of the living bread in thanks. This is never done, to my knowledge, with other baked goods—cakes, pies, cookies, biscuits. Only bread is so honored. When the Temple stood in Jerusalem, every Shabbat the priests placed loaves of bread upon the altar.

Barley and wheat are indigenous to the Middle East. Barley was probably the first grain to be cultivated, since it thrives in poor soil and dry conditions, standard for our ancestors. Since barley ripened and was harvested before wheat, barley flour was believed to be the original flour used for the ceremonial Pesach matzot. Wheat became popular later, once it was improved so it was easier to harvest. Barley made simple flat cakes and porridge and the same kind of pilaf dishes we can make with it today, and it could be fermented into beer, but it wasn't so great for leavened bread.

Matzoh, not allowed to ferment, feels far more inert in the hand and also purer than bread. It is "just" flour and water, nothing more, nothing less, simple and with little flavor. It is the essence of bread, bread in its purest and most basic form. You strip out the sweetening agents, the leavening, the seeds or fruit; you leave out any fat or oil. No spices, no herbs. Just flour and water and heat. Yet we say not only the blessing for bread, the hamotzi, but we then particularly bless the matzoh itself. These blessings and suggestions for others are in chapter 4.

Matzoh

Flat you are as a doormat
and as homely.
No crust, no glaze, you lack
a cosmetic glow.
You break with a snap.
You are dry as a twig
split from an oak
in midwinter.
You are bumpy as a mud basin
in a drought.
Square as a slab of pavement,
you have no inside
to hide raisins or seeds.
You are pale as the full moon
pocked with craters.

What we see is what we get,
honest, plain, dry
shining with nostalgia
as if baked with light
instead of heat.
The bread of flight and haste
in the mouth you
promise, home.

You might view matzoh as defined by negatives: what it does not contain, what is not permitted in or around it, all that it is not.

You might see it as the bread of poverty. At this season, we revisit our history—recalled by matzoh, as the bread taken by fleeing Israelites when they had no time to prepare for the journey into the wilderness. It is described as *lechem oni,* the bread of affliction, the sustenance of slaves, the minimum of what might continue life awhile, yet it is also the bread of freedom, of those who chose to leave slavery and flee into danger and a totally new life as a nation.

Matzoh is the bread of haste. If you aren't prepared when an opportunity comes for liberation, for action, then you must take it anyhow. The people had no provisions prepared, the Torah tells us, but they had one chance for liberty. So they went with only the bread of haste. If you delay, if you procrastinate, even if you simply want to be totally ready before you act, then you will probably lose the moment in which you might act. Think of the Jews who were not ready to leave Germany. They had affairs to put in order. They had things they had to accomplish, arrangements to make. So they stayed and then the opportunity to escape was gone. Matzoh tells us to leap when we have to, lest we be eaten. Leaping into the unknown is not comfortable, but it may be the only option for preserving or gaining your freedom.

You might see it as the purest of all breads. It cannot distract us from our mission on this night, to experience the Exodus as if we were truly a part of it, as the traditional haggadah bids us, to experience our cultural and spiritual group identity and to examine it. We are trying to strip ourselves this night of all the nonsense programmed into us by the media, by advertising in all its varied and intrusive forms, of concerns our egos churn up: Are we pretty enough, esteemed enough, popular enough? Do we have enough things to qualify as successful in the eyes of ourselves, our family, our neighbors, our colleagues? Are we getting ahead—of whom, of what, and why?

You might think of matzoh as an example to emulate for that night: get to the essence of something you choose to examine: perhaps it is the essence of being a Jew and what it means for you and for your family. Perhaps you want to contemplate your own oppression, your own inner or outer Egypt. During the seder, some years when we finish the Maggid, I urge participants to ask themselves about what forms their personal Egypt: a kind of addiction, not necessarily physical; a kind of self-deprecation or self-doubt they have carried since childhood or adolescence; some aspect of their personality or behavior that holds them back from being a better person or doing what they believe they might be capable of—for instance, the habit of envying other people their luck or success or simply the attention paid them. It might be a situation into which the person has come and remains—an unfulfilling or oppressive job; a bad relationship; a codependency that is hurting both parties. Only the individual knows what personal Egypt—Mitzrayim, which means in Hebrew "the narrow place"—he or she is stuck in. One year, I e-mailed the participants ahead of time and asked them to bring a picture or object that represented something in each of their lives they wished to change or leave.

Maybe you long to make room in your life for some spiritual practice: Maybe you want to start keeping Shabbat, whenever you can; maybe you simply want to light the candles, say the blessings, have a Shabbat dinner with those you love, sing a few songs. Maybe you always meant to start meditating. Maybe you want to find a way to go to services that speak to you, even if it means "synagogue shopping." Maybe you want to study Torah, but have never given it the time it would take. Maybe you want to make *aliyah* to Israel, but you keep putting it off. Maybe you want to study kabbalah with a good teacher, but none has ever grabbed you by the elbow and dragged you off.

Some years I ask people to think about that narrow place in community or societal terms. Who or what is getting squeezed? I ask them to think about *tikkun olam*, the repair of the world. What could each of them decide to do in the next year to make the society less oppressive, less confining—to widen out the narrow place in which we or others are caught. What action can we take? How can we put some of our energy, our resources, our time and caring to work? So we deliberate on the matzoh as suggesting in its simplicity something we could strip away from ourselves or the world.

Matzoh was the bread of poverty. Do we still have the poor with us? Have any of us ever been poor, even briefly? What did it feel like? How do we think of the poor in our own society? How do we view poverty—as a social disease, as a calamity, as an inherited situation or trait, as a sign of moral weakness or decay? In our own society, poor people have endured all of these stigmas. How do you imagine someone might "escape" from poverty? How could it be erased? Or do you think of it as a natural condition of "others."

We have in essence a quiet bread, a bread of silence, a bread of nothing much. This is all I am; eat me and think, What are you? If you can get *matzoh shemura*, it is even more so. It feels like a handmade artifact. But any *matzoh kosher l'Pesach*, kosher for

Passover, is fine. Now, matzoh is the bread of haste in more than one way. Do not only think of our ancestors rushing to flee Egypt but think of the process of making matzoh for Pesach: it must be made completely within eighteen minutes so that there is no time for the yeasts that are ambient, that float in the air, to enter the simple dough. Everything that touches it must be constantly cleaned, to avoid contamination. The bread of haste, in its creation, in the moment of action, of revolt, of becoming refugees: the food they carried with them as so many people fleeing war or oppression flee with what food they can grab to carry; as our immigrant ancestors carried food with them when they journeyed across the oceans in steerage to these or other shores. By the way, before it became okay to make the matzoh by machine, matzoh was made by hand, of course, and it was round. The first matzoh mentioned in Torah is made by Sarah and served to the three strangers, messengers from the Eternal. It is described as round.

You need three matzot for the seder's leader. You can put them on the seder plate if you have an unusually large one or one that has tiers. Otherwise, it's easier to take a separate plate to display them. You want a matzoh cover—some way to separate the three of them from one another, or at least something to cover the whole plate. Some communities separate the matzot; others cover the three of them together. Jewish artifact shops sell matzoh covers and often people make one for themselves. They are as pretty as you want them to be and usually have the Hebrew word *matzoh* embroidered on them. You can, by the way, use either a special seder plate or whatever suitable platter you have.

The middle matzoh will be broken into two parts—

intentionally uneven, one bigger, one smaller. After the Karpas is dipped in salt water and eaten, the leader shows the matzoh and then divides it. The smaller part goes back onto the plate, between the two whole matzot and under the cover. The larger piece is the afikomen, which the leader hides. Breaking the matzoh divides its two meanings: the smaller piece is matzoh as the bread of slavery, of misery; the large piece is the bread of freedom. Traditionally, the leader reclined and put the afikomen under his pillow. In modern times, kids expect to search for the matzoh and receive a reward. The way we do it, I am leading the seder but my husband takes the afikomen and while we are otherwise engaged, he hides it. The kids try to watch him but he always fools them. They have never caught him hiding the afikomen. Some years he hides it too well, and we have to give clues when the search is dragging on too long. It is important to confine the hiding to two or three rooms. We keep the search downstairs, where the dining room is. It cannot be hidden out of reach of the smallest child who will be looking for it. In other families, the children try to steal the afikomen. Then the leader must ransom it back.

Remember that you need lots of matzoh handy for people to use first for the matzoh that is eaten alone and then for their Hillel sandwich of Charoset, Maror, and matzoh (some people only do the Maror and the matzoh and not the Charoset for the Hillel sandwich) and for the meal as well. The upper matzoh is usually said to represent freedom, and the remnant of the middle matzoh stands for slavery. When you chew them together, you are supposed to be converting slavery into freedom. Some of the imagery of the seder is a bit elusive. That particular bit of symbolism has never worked for me, but it does for some people.

The matzoh for the meal you can simply place in the middle of the table. The blessing early in the seder over the matzot blesses all of it. We also like to include, as do a number of contemporary seders, the prayer of the Jews of Bergen-Belsen from 1944. This is my shortened rendering of it.

Eternal One, You know that it's our desire to do your will and celebrate the festival of Pesach by eating matzoh and by shunning leavened food. We are in pain that being slaves prevents us from keeping your command-ments and we are besides in danger of dying. Observe that we are eager and ready to fulfill your commandments: "And you will live by them and not die by them." We pray that you may keep us alive and preserve and redeem us soon so that we may observe your laws with perfect hearts. Amein.

You might want to say this after the feast in the third section of the haggadah, but I like it with the matzoh.

Okay, Pesach seders are over and done with but you have lots of matzoh left that you don't particularly feel like eating. Maybe you use it with meals, but there is no obligation to eat any more of it. What do you do with it, besides feed it to the birds (who do appreciate it, by the way)? How about breakfast or lunch matzoh brei, for instance? When I told Ira I was going to explain how to cook matzoh brei, he thought I was crazy. Everybody knows how to make matzoh brei, he said. But I am of the opinion that there is no longer anything that everybody knows how to cook.

Matzoh Brei

This is a loose recipe, subject to many variations to which you can freely add.

Beat 2 eggs for each 2 *matzot*. Some people add milk or milk and water.

Crumble matzoh or break into small pieces and add to beaten eggs. Now you have a choice: salty or sweet. You can cut up some lox or add minced onion. Let the matzoh sit for a while to absorb the egg.

Or you can make it without lox or onions, then serve it with jam. Same procedure: Soak before cooking. Sprinkle with cinnamon after you turn it.

Heat oil or butter or a combination in a frying pan. Get it hot, then put in the mixture and turn down the heat. Cook for 6 to 8 minutes, turn it like a pancake and cook until lightly browned Serve warm. Sour cream is good with it. Some people like applesauce or honey.

I like it eggier, rather than on the dry side. Just experiment. I especially enjoy it for breakfast.

◎

Remember: there is a recipe for making tzimmes in chapter 2, using farfel, which is just little pieces of matzoh. You can easily make your own farfel.

Here's a main dish using up matzoh:

◎

Eggplant Burgers

1 pound ground beef, preferably lean
1 small onion or half a yellow one, minced
Oregano or basil
Salt and pepper to taste
1 egg for mixture
2 tablespoons matzoh meal
2 to 3 tablespoons fresh parsley, finely minced
3 or 4 cloves minced garlic
1 eggplant, peeled

Preheat the oven to 375°F.

Mix the chopped beef thoroughly with the onion, oregano and/or basil, salt, pepper, egg, matzoh meal, parsley, and garlic. Make sure the other ingredients are mixed well through the chopped beef.

Sauté it briefly.

Slice the eggplant into ½ inch circles. Sauté the slices in olive oil in two or three batches. You are not cooking them thoroughly, but just about halfway. Form burgers and place each between two slices of eggplant.
Bake on greased cookie sheet for about 30 minutes. They are delicious.

◎

Here's a dairy dish.

◎

Matzot with Cottage Cheese #1

4 eggs
6 matzot
1 pound small-curd cottage cheese
2 tablespoons melted unsalted butter
½ teaspoon cinnamon
⅓ cup raisins or sultanas (you could also make this with cut-up dried apricots)
1 tablespoon brown sugar
¼ teaspoon salt

Preheat the oven to 350°F.

Beat 2 eggs, then break the matzoh into quarters and soak them in the eggs.

In a separate bowl, beat 2 more eggs and then add everything else, including the cottage cheese.

Grease a baking dish. Put a layer of the egg-soaked matzoh in the bottom, cover it with the layer of the cottage cheese mixture, then another layer of matzoh, and so on.

Bake for 30 minutes.

This makes 6 to 8 servings.

◎

Stale matzoh is not the world's most exciting nosh, so I recommend using it up.

Now if you made matzoh balls (recipe in chapter 18), you probably have leftover matzoh meal. If so, here is a good use for it.

◎

Chremslach

You can make these simply with eggs and matzoh meal and maybe a little milk.

Beat 2 eggs first, then add a little salt and matzoh meal to make enough of a consistency to hold together. If you like, you can add a little fat or oil. Cook the pancakes on a griddle or in a frying pan.

You can also get fancier, adding raisins or currants or cut-up dried apricots. You can add allspice or ginger or cinnamon. You can add sugar or a little maple syrup. Basically you're making pancakes and you can do anything you like with them.

If you have a waffle iron, you can also make waffles with the same recipe.

◎

As an accompaniment to stew or soup or meat tzimmes or *cholent*, you can make knaidlach. These resemble matzoh balls but are bigger and heavier and usually sliced at the end of cooking.

◎

Matzoh Knaidlach

You make this when you are making the soup, the stew, or the cholent or tzimmes.

Beat 2 or 3 eggs, then add ¼ cup rendered goose or chicken fat. If you are avoiding that kind of fat, you can use olive oil, a bit less. Work 1¾ to 2 cups of matzoh meal into the fat and the eggs. Then work in the seasonings: salt, pepper, any herbs you want to use: thyme is good, so are fines herbs, fresh parsley, or a little ground sage.

This is one of those inexact recipes. You want the balls to cohere—not to be too loose or too dry. You can add a little more fat or oil or you can add more matzoh meal. Form it into a ball or a long sausage shape. Then you float it on top of the rest of the meal and let it cook slowly.

◎

I don't make knaidlach on Pesach itself because we are having matzoh balls in the chicken soup. I make it later in the week, when I need to use up matzoh meal. We always buy more matzoh meal than we need in case something should go wrong with the matzoh balls in the soup, and we should have to make more of them.

Here's another use for leftover matzoh.

◎

Sweet Pancakes

6 matzot
4 large eggs
⅓ cup chopped almonds (use a food processor very lightly so you don't grind them up)
Some raisins or currants or chopped-up dried apricots
1 tablespoon dried lemon peel or 2 tablespoons fresh lemon zest
1 tablespoon olive oil or canola oil
Olive or canola oil for the griddle or frying pan

SAUCE
⅔ cup honey
1 tablespoon lemon juice
Orange juice or liqueur to taste

Soak the matzot in cold water until soft. Then squeeze
the water out of them. You want to end up with about
3 cups of matzot squeezed and pressed into a measuring
cup. In a large bowl, combine the matzot, eggs, almonds,
dried fruit, and lemon zest. Then add 1 tablespoon oil.
Mix well.

Heat the oil in a large frying pan. Drop the batter in as
you would for smallish pancakes. Cook it over moderate
heat, turning it when it's golden on the bottom. When
this batch is done, just as you would for regular
pancakes, take them out, keep them warm, and continue.
Or go to the table with this batch, eat, and then go back
and do another batch, taking care that the oil does not
burn and smoke. You can always add more oil.

While the first batch is cooking, in a small pan heat the
honey and lemon juice, and you can add water, orange
juice, or any type of liqueur you would like to use—
perhaps Cointreau or Grand Marnier, perhaps Kahlua,
perhaps rum or brandy, although they are not kosher.
Your choice. This sauce only cooks for a couple of
minutes until thoroughly warm and the honey is
dissolved in the liquid. Serve it with the pancakes.

◎

Near the end of chapter 2, "Chametz," there's another recipe for using up leftover matzot, a hearty family dish in which the matzoh is turned into a little pie filled with ground lamb or beef. In chapter 19, "The Feast," there are more recipes for using matzoh.

I don't mind giving the matzoh farfel to the birds, but I hate not to use up the *kosher l'Pesach matzot* and the matzoh meal. So I wax inventive during the rest of Pesach. If you have enough for the seder or seders, then you will always have leftover matzoh.

THE AFIKOMEN

After the meal, the children search for the afikomen. My husband hides the afikomen well, so that the search is real. We always have a gift of chocolate in some special form for the winner and smaller treats for all the children who searched. One problem has been a cutoff age. We have teenagers who have searched for the afikomen since they were five and who want to take part with the little kids, which isn't fair. You need to work out the house rules beforehand. At some seders, the ransom is paid in money to donate to some charity that feeds the poor or homeless.

When the afikomen is returned to the leader at the end of the meal—after dessert—everyone eats a tiny piece. We always say that the afikomen shows us how even what appears to be lost or separated from us can be restored if we do not forget it and if we really search for it. *Afikomen* does not sound like a Hebrew word; its origin is Greek and means "dessert" or what ends the meal.

Make sure everyone gets a piece. Sometimes people save a bit of the afikomen for good luck, as it was believed to have strong mystical powers, able to avert shipwreck or to guard against disease. Sometimes a piece of that year's afikomen was placed in a house to protect it. In any event, what was whole is first broken, then hidden, then found and redeemed by the leader of the seder. You can play with the symbolism of this and find new meanings if you like. At your seder, you can use the breaking of the afikomen or its hiding and recovery to raise questions and launch discussion. Perhaps everyone present will find something a little different in the adventures of the afikomen.

It accentuates the part of the seder that is not remembering, not thanking, but searching. We search for what we need to change in ourselves and in our world. We search for a way to connect with our history. We search for meaning in all the items on the seder plate and in all the parts of the haggadah we are using. The larger piece that is hidden may symbolize to you how much we have yet to find, how much we still must try to understand.

It is also a time to reflect on the meaning of "hidden" in our history and experience. In the story of the Exodus, Yocheved, the mother of Moses, hides her baby boy for three months so he will not be killed. Miriam hides in the reeds to watch the fate of her brother. Miriam hides her identity as the baby's sister, and Yocheved hides her identity as she serves as nurse to her own son. Moses's identity as a Hebrew is hidden.

Jews have often had to hide their identity. In Spain and Portugal, Jews who did not or were not able to flee the Inquisition had to hide their Jewishness or they would die horribly from torture. Many of them hid their identities so well, even from their children, that only now are some of their descendents learning that their ancestors were Jews—I know of cases in New Bedford where families had the tradition of going down in the basement on Friday night, lighting candles, and saying some gibberish they didn't understand. Why? Because their parents and grandparents did that and told them to. I have read recently of cases from New Mexico. There, some people are trying to help others find out if their ancestors were Jews, which brings them to the decision of whether to identify as Jews and live as Jews—which some have begun to do. There was a whole tribe of Black Jews in South Africa whose DNA proves they are Jews as they say, but who were cut off for millennia from the rest of Jewry. Only recently have they been "found"—identified and sent teachers and rabbis.

Under the Nazis, Jews had to hide physically and/or hide their children disguised as Christians among the gentile population. Have you ever hidden—pretended not to be a Jew or simply not identified as a Jew when someone was making anti-Semitic remarks? Or when someone was telling JAP (Jewish American Princess) jokes or simply using a phrase like "jewing me down on the price"? Ask at the seder table about such experiences; the results may be unsettling. It can put you in touch with your heritage in a frightening way.

Unlike most African-Americans (although not all), we have a choice sometimes about identifying ourselves—sometimes not. Sometimes we are recognized by those who dislike or even hate Jews. Many Jews coming to the United States changed their names to escape the identification. Generations of up-and-coming Jews gave their children non-Jewish names like "Sanford" and "Sheldon," which shortly afterward became identified as Jewish names, too, as much as "Itzak" and "Feygeleh" and "Hymie" had been. Sometimes Jews hid their identities in order to get a job. When I went job hunting in high school, my mother would say to me, "Put down 'Protestant' instead of 'Jewish,' unless they're Jews, or they won't hire you." I grew up in Detroit when the housing covenants against African-Americans and Jews were in full force, preventing us from renting or buying in most neighborhoods.

So the notion of being "hidden" can mean many things to us. Finding meanings in symbols may require much searching. Our history, even our family histories, may have been obfuscated and require us to become very private detectives to ferret out the past. I have met children of survivors who for years knew little or nothing of their parents' past—in one case, a woman did not know that she had a sibling who had died at Auschwitz, long before her birth. As we each eat a little piece of the afikomen and move back toward the haggadah and the last two sections of the seder, we might want to discuss with one another the meanings of "hidden" and "found" or "reclaimed" as some of us are reclaiming a Judaism we may have grown estranged from or misplaced or never really explored before.

One year you might want to lead into a discussion of "hidden." Another year, you might focus on "search," in our lives and our history. Still another year, you might focus on the meaning of "finding" or "found." How do we search and for what? Is what we find always what we were searching for, or thought we were? What are the ways in which we seek meaning in our lives? How "found" does something remain, once located, if it is not used or does not continue to grow or develop?

12
Maror

*M*aror is translated as "bitter herbs." It is one of the three items whose meaning must, according to Rabbi Gameliel, be included in the seder: matzoh, the shank bone standing in for the Paschal lamb of Temple sacrifice, and the bitter herbs.

In Ashkenazi usage, horseradish is often used. I have also seen romaine used, but that seems strange to me. Unless it has bolted—which it would never have done by the time of Pesach— it is not at all bitter. Bitter is obviously a problem, since we don't eat bitter things—sweet, salty, sour, spicy, hot, but not bitter. I presume there were herbs available in the Middle East that were bitter but edible. Rue is an herb on the bitter side, but some people have a bad reaction to it. Aspirin is certainly bitter and mentioned as such in the Lamentations of Jeremiah; however, I can't imagine putting it on the seder plate. Wormwood is used as a metaphor for bitter, but I think it is unwise to consume it: absinthe was banned because it contained an infusion of wormwood. Chicory can be quite bitter. Perhaps it could be used, but it might be confused with Chazeret or Karpas. Hops are bitter (hence the term for beer brewed with a lot of them), but again, a bottle of bitters on the seder plate is hardly appropriate, and ale or beer are full of leaven. So we seem to be stuck with horseradish.

Some years ago, I tried to grow horseradish. It certainly grows well here, but getting large roots that are easy to grate requires as much soil preparation as a rosebush or rhubarb. Plus the roots were never big enough by Pesach for me to use them, so I'd have to buy it anyhow. I decided to give up, but the horseradish did not agree. I have a patch of it I tried to eradicate. Now I have surrendered to its superior vigor. Sometimes I use the roots in the fall, with cole crops like broccoli. What I have discovered is that horseradish produces lovely yellow blooms in early summer that have a pleasant fragrance. I often add it to bouquets. I enjoy asking guests to identify the flowers.

For Pesach, I buy both the red and the white horseradish in their bottles and heap each in a pretty bowl, so that those who like it strong can have the white and those who like it mellower can use the red. By the way, if you do decide to grate your own horseradish, don't do it by hand and be careful when you lift the lid on your food processor. It will give your sinuses a real jolt. Once you've ground the horseradish, stand well back and add vinegar and a bit of salt. Then turn it on again. Some people serve chunks of raw horseradish so that the bitter kick can be as strong as possible. To me, that borders on sadism, especially with small children. There's sometimes a macho contest among the guys at the table to show who can eat the hottest and bitterest horseradish.

Horseradish was obviously not the original bitter herb, since it's native to Europe, although it traveled early. The Egyptians and the Greeks were familiar with it; however, it's hard for me to equate familiarity with their notion that it was an aphrodisiac. It owes its current usage mostly to Central Europe. From Germany, its culinary uses spread into Eastern Europe, north into Scandinavia and west into Great Britain. Early settlers brought it with them to New England, where it sometimes grows wild. It's said to have excellent properties as a liniment and to be good for digestion and as an expectorant and cough medicine. There's a museum devoted to horseradish in Bavaria.

Bitter herbs: so we make do with what we can conveniently acquire. Bitter because we are bidden to remember the oppression of our ancestors in slavery, no doubt worked to death much like the able-bodied (in the beginning) Jews worked to death for Farben, for Krups and other corporations. Bitter because there is much in life that is bitter. Some we can change; some we can't. We need to remember pain, slavery, prejudice, the weariness of those without hope so that we can empathize with them in a useful manner and then work to change what we can that causes that bitterness. If we spend too much time contemplating our own bitterness, we may feel comfortable as victims and see ourselves as too injured to bother with other people's problems.

Maror

A bitter cud.
Biting into the bitter, that bites back.
Of all the gross tastes, sweet and salty,

sour, we seek it the least.
We spit it out. But not tonight.

Tonight we must taste our bitterness.
Bite into our failure, suck its essence.
We were slaves in Egypt, the hagaddah
reminds us, and we still are,
but who enslaves us to what?

The bone we chew is our own.
Only I can tell myself where
I am caught, trapped, held
fast, bored but comfortable
in the box I know so well.

This is the moment for naming
that box, for feeling the walls,
for studying the dimensions
of the prison I must choose
to leave in my exodus of one.

I can join with no one else,
I cannot walk out with you
until I measure my walls
then break them down.
Darkness into light.

Fear and silence into
cursing. The known
abandoned for something
new and frightening. Bitter
is the first taste of freedom.

The Pesach season is a good time to think about our lives. Of course, we are bidden to do so during the Days of Awe, but at Pesach as winter fades away and the world opens up, we might think about how we can free ourselves from what confines us and how we can make our society and our world freer for everyone, how we can end our own and others' oppression. Only when we understand our bitterness can we move out from it. We all know people who spend their lives complaining about and resenting something in their past—that their mother or father didn't love them enough, that they didn't have certain objects or experiences they desired or wish that they had been able to have, that they didn't go to the right school or make certain career choices early on, that someone they desired or fell in love with never loved them back. They know their bitterness but they have not assimilated it and moved on. They are still caught in the oppression of their own private Egypt. Unless we can get out of our narrow place, we will remain there all of our lives, embittered and embittering. Some of us have truly been victims, but to remain so if we survive is to deny ourselves our potential. We must recognize the pain and then, as we can, let go.

Rabbi Zalman Schachter-Shalomi has suggested that the pain of eating bitterness is sometimes instructive. We can learn through pain. Pain suggests to us that something is wrong that needs to be fixed. What is wrong must come to our attention before we can make it right.

At some seders, participants eat the matzoh with the bitter herbs before adding the Charoset. At others, the Hillel sandwich of matzoh, Charoset, and Maror is eaten to fulfill the obligation of eating bitter herbs. Your choice. But I recommend you attempt to explore together the meaning of bitterness. It may prove very useful in the long run to the people around your table.

Think about the victims of war, of demeaning and enslaving customs, of people who do not even have bitter herbs to fill their stomachs, of people dying of AIDs, of malaria, of cholera, of a hundred preventable and curable diseases that are not prevented and are not cured. Why? Think of people whose homes are destroyed, think of people uprooted because of their religion or ethnicity, think of people killed because of who they are, not what they ever have done, blown apart by terrorist bombs or bombed by armies who label themselves liberators. Do they deserve to be bitter? Is it just that they hate people who had nothing to do with that disaster? What if they pass on their bitterness to their children? When will it ever stop?

I have spent much of my life contemplating the bitterness many women experience, the sense of being compressed, denied, ignored, wanting much and getting little, wanting little and getting nothing, forced into economic or sexual slavery. For all the women who eat bitterness every day of their lives, I take my share of bitter herbs and remember. I think of my grandmother who bore eleven children in poverty; I think of my mother yearning after meaning and enlightenment, who had to leave school in the tenth grade to go to work as a chambermaid; I think of my aunt whose first husband beat her; I think of my friend who died of a botched abortion when controlling her own body was illegal for a woman. I taste the bitterness of their oppression and rededicate myself to doing more to erase that pain from the world.

Eating the bitter herbs, we move from experiencing our own oppression to considering and feeling the oppression of others— and we begin to think about which particular oppression we will work to change, so that one tiny shred of bitterness may vanish from the world. *Tikkun olam:* repair of the world.

The task never completed

No task is ever completed,
only abandoned or pressed into use.
Tinkering can be a form of prayer.

Twenty-six botched worlds preceded
Genesis, we are told in ancient commentary,
and Hashem said not only,

of this particular attempt
It is good, but muttered,
if only it will hold.

Incomplete, becoming, the world
was given us to fix, to complete
and we've almost worn it out.

My house was hastily built,
on the cheap. Leaks, rotting
sills, the floor a relief map of Idaho,

Whenever I get some money, I stove
up, repair, add on, replace.
This improvisation permits me to squat

here on the land that owns me.
We evolve through mistakes, wrong
genes, imitation gone wild,

Each night sleep unravels me into wool,
then into sheep and wolf. Walls and fire
pass through me. I birth stones.

Every dawn I stumble from the roaring
vat of dreams and make myself up
remembering and forgetting by halves.

Every dawn I choose to take a knife
to the world's flank or a sewing kit,
rough improvisation, but a start.

You might ask people sitting around your seder table what they can do in pursuit of that repair of the world and to erase bitterness from some little part of it. If we could have "bitter herbs" instead of the horseradish we substitute for whatever the herbs were originally, the symbolism would be stronger. Herbs are temporary. They wilt or dry up. Even when we intentionally dry them, they last only a few months before they lose their savor. So the bitterness we are contemplating can be temporary also, if only we work to make it so. But we have to consider what we are really willing to do to diminish the sum of bitterness in the world—what small task can we take on? What pledge can we make to ease some pain or fight some oppression?

I found a Sephardic recipe for consuming bitter herbs at

Passover in a dish, if you want to go that way. You might want to have this as a first course, after the ritual eating of the bitter herbs with matzoh.

◎

Passover Green Salad

You need romaine, chicory, endive—you could easily substitute Belgian endive for the usual green kind, as it has a stronger taste. You need fresh parsley—you probably bought a great big bunch for Karpas anyhow.

You need arugula or watercress or peppergrass. If Pesach is late enough in the spring that year, you might well have arugula and peppergrass out of your garden by then. I usually do if it's past mid-April.

You need fresh mint and dill or cilantro—some mixture of these fresh herbs.

You need some form of onion. Shallots or scallions would be good, or you could use a red onion. Slice the onions thin. Then add them to the greens. Add the herbs.

For the dressing: Crush fresh garlic. Add olive oil, lemon juice, salt, and pepper, and mix well. When ready to serve, add the dressing to the greens.

If you serve plain boiled eggs to begin the meal, this might be a good accompaniment.

◎

*C*hazeret is the most neglected item on the seder plate. If you Google Charoset, you get too many entries to check—hundreds of recipes, lots of reminiscences of childhood seders and family customs. The very mention of Charoset seems to conjure up good feelings and warm sentiment. If you Google Chazeret, you get *two* entries. Partly, lettuce seems there almost by accident. Wild lettuce was one of the original possibilities for Maror. Some Ashkenazim do not put Chazeret on the seder plate at all. In most Ashkenazi and Sephardic usage, Chazeret takes its own place, whatever that is. Its presence seems to have something to do with "greens" or "herbs" in the Hebrew being a plural, so that some rabbis thought there should be more than one on the seder plate.

But mystery is the essence of the seder. You have to provide your own explanation of the presence of matzoh instead of normal bread, of Maror instead of broccoli or spinach, of Karpas dipped into salt water. You are presented with the ritual items and sometimes there is a brief explanation and sometimes there is none, so you have to tease out the meanings according to your own values and experiences. You have to create the meaning in the symbol. In a good seder everybody gets to ask questions and everybody gets to contribute to the understanding.

Wild lettuce (*Lactuca scariola*) grew in the Near East in Iran and Turkistan, a tall rangy plant with bitter leaves. (I have selected this species name from several. There seems to be disagreement as to the correct botanical name for wild lettuce.) Egyptian hieroglyphics indicate some kind of lettuce was cultivated there by 2000 BCE. By the sixth century BCE, lettuce was grown and served in Persia. As it was tamed and bred, it became *Lactuca sativa*, the various forms of lettuce cultivars we are familiar with. It rapidly conquered Greece and then Rome. By Roman times, many types of lettuce had been bred and intense cultivation continued in the Middle Ages and on to the present. Some authorities recognize it in Egyptian tombs, not in the wild form, but as Cos lettuce (the tall upright loosely constructed heads with dark green or reddish leaves). Augustus Caesar erected a statue to Romaine, the favored kind in Rome—hence its name. Lettuce came to the New World with Columbus; settlers from Europe brought strains for their kitchen gardens. Thomas Jefferson grew nineteen kinds at Monticello. Yes, lettuce marched on and on, conquering the salad plate only to die a humiliating death in America by being turned into iceberg lettuce, grown by the carload and tasting like a salad of crunchy newspapers.

Lettuce is so easy to grow that if you have any space outdoors or even in a window box or on a balcony, you might want to plant some. As a bonus, most types are pretty, especially the red varieties. The best prepackaged varieties of lettuce you can buy are inferior to lettuce a child of seven can grow in a space the size of a sandbox. You can even stick lettuce plants in a flower bed and they blend well. Since I don't have a greenhouse, I, too, am dependent on the plastic wrapped stuff from the supermarket mid-December through mid-April, but I know what I'm missing. What you can't do with lettuce is preserve it—not by canning, not by freezing, not by dehydrating it. You eat it fresh or you don't eat it at all. Like many things in life, you enjoy it at once or it spoils. You could see this as a symbol for the opportunities that arise for change and are quickly gone.

Mostly we take lettuce for granted. It's there in the supermarket all year long. If you eat iceberg lettuce, then you assume that lettuce has no flavor. Check the dressings aisle: giving the tasteless some kind of flavor is big business. Personally, I grow six lettuce varieties in spring, one or two heat-resistant varieties in summer, and in fall, some that bear cold well (like Brune D'Hiver and Winter Density Cos). All the lettuces I grow have flavor, and some exhibit beautiful red color. Seldom can I harvest lettuce by the time of Pesach, unless it is well into April. Then I can use my own lettuce, usually Salad Bowl. It's not my favorite, but it's the easiest to start inside and move outside well before the last frost, under milk cartons or agricultural cloth. The darker the green, the more food value you get for your lettuce—and superior flavor.

Chazeret

Bland almost as water,
you are meek and prolific as mice.

You are the carrier of sharp news,
a pretense for dressing you up,
a hanger, a clothes horse,
but with a certain shy sweetness.

You sit there demurely in the garden
rows with almost no pests.
Then one day you stick up
a tower of leaves
and turn bitter overnight,
sculptured, tall, inedible.

You have escaped us:
our sharp teeth and our salad
bowls, our sandwiches and rolls.
Instead like a green rocket you rise
hot and spiky, joyfully bitter
waving your own new flag.

I have heard lettuce on the seder plate explained as representing what happens to those who remain in slavery too long and turn bitter. If the lettuce remains too long in the garden, it becomes strongly flavored and inedible—bitter, again. If we do not try to escape a bad situation, we will embitter ourselves. The parallelism suggests that we will become nasty, infected by our situation. But of course if we see the lettuce bolting, we also see that it is trying to go to seed—to reproduce itself, to spread its genes so that its descendants survive and flourish. So the bitterness that our taste buds experience, to the lettuce is not death but survival of the line—the lettuce preparing to give birth to the seeds of its progeny. Bolting is fruition and ripeness for the lettuce. For us, it is the turning of a vegetable into a weed. However, weeds have the superior ability to survive and reproduce. They flourish where our cultivated delicate overbred plants perish from drought or excessive rain or insect depredation. So lettuce in its flowering liberates itself from our needs and meets its own.

Lettuce, by the way, is a natural soporific. Its milky sap was in the past processed into "lettuce opium" and used as a sedative. So don't eat too much Chazeret before you get to the meal.

The love of lettuce

With a pale green curly
lust I gloat over it nestled
there on the wet earth
(oak leaf, buttercrunch, ruby, cos)
like so many nests
waiting for birds
who lay hard-boiled eggs.

The first green eyes
of the mustard, the frail
wands of carrots, the fat
thrust of the peas: all
are precious as I kneel
in the mud weeding
and the thinnings go into the salad.

The garden with crooked
wandering rows dug
by the two of us
drunk with sunshine has
an intricate pattern emerging
like the back of a rug.
The tender seedlings

raise their pinheads
with the cap of seed stuck on.
Cruel and smiling with sharp
teeth is the love of lettuce.
You grow out of last year's
composted dinner and you
will end in my hot mouth.

Rather than face horseradish eaten with matzoh or with matzoh and Charoset, some people use Chazeret in its place to make the Hillel sandwich. So take your choice. You can have your Chazeret and eat it, too, standing in for bitter herbs.

14
Charoset

Who doesn't love Charoset? A gentile friend once said to me, "Why do you only make it once a year? It tastes so good. You ought to serve it often. It's the Jewish guacamole." But I am never tempted and I don't know any Jew who makes it except at Pesach. It's special because it contrasts so strongly with the other ritual items, the matzoh, the Maror, the Karpas—bland or bitter or pungent. You don't want to have it any other time, because it belongs to that ritual, that meal, that week, marking the occasion.

Charoset

Sweet and sticky
I always make too much
at Pesach so I have
an excuse to eat you
all week.

Moist and red
the female treat
nothing at all like clay
for bricks, nothing
like mortar.

No, you are sweet as
a mouth kissing,
you are fragrant
with cinnamon
spicy as havdalah boxes.

Don't go on too long,
you whisper sweetly.
Heed the children
growing restive, their
bellies growling.

You speak of pleasure
in the midst of remembered pain
You offer the first taste
of the meal, promising joy
like a picnic on a stone

where long ago an ancestor
was buried, too long
ago to weep. We nod
and remembering is enough
to offer, like honey.

If much of what we must
recall is bitter, you
are the reminder that
joy too lights its candles
tonight in the mind.

Charoset had no part in the original Pesach, only the required bitter herbs, matzoh, and the shank bone and/or roasted egg to stand for the Paschal lamb, the Temple sacrifice. At some point in the distant past, rabbis added Charoset to have something sweet to offset the bitter herbs. A good idea. Who doesn't love Charoset? I guess the cats don't eat it, although one of my cats did taste it last year, the Abyssinian who eats pumpkin, papayas, mangoes, and cantaloupe. He nibbled a little with pleasure.

There are as many recipes for Charoset as there are Jews who do anything in the kitchen. Basically they fall into four categories: your standard Ashkenazi and its variations; your Sephardic and its variations; Mizraki variations; and recipes produced by foodies and cookbook writers who want to do something original. All of them are combinations of various fruits, some kind of nuts, spices, and sweet wine or something else sweet. I'll give you a few recipes but you can create your own from what you have on hand or feel inspired to add. These recipes can give you a sense of the possibilities. It should be fun. You can chop by hand, using a mezzaluna or sharp knives; you can, as I do, use a food processor, but with a light hand. If you don't just keep hitting the pulse button quickly and then letting go, you will make mush. I do the nuts first, then the whole cinnamon sticks and bits of fresh ginger if I use that, and then I add the other ingredients. Charoset is supposed to be kind of chunky, not pureed. If you have too fine a consistency, you end up with just weird fruit sauce. I never make it exactly the same way two years running.

Here's a fairly standard Ashkenazi recipe.

◎

Ashkenazi Charoset

4 to 5 large apples, peeled, cored, and chopped
2 cups chopped walnuts
2 teaspoons ground cinnamon
4 tablespoons kosher sweet red wine
Sugar to taste

Mix the chopped apples, nuts, and cinnamon together in a bowl. Then add the wine and sugar. Mix thoroughly, taste, and refrigerate until you are ready for the seder.

◎

Apples are the commonest fruit in Ashkenazi Charoset. For one thing, some kinds keep well in storage and thus would be available at Pesach time in Northern Europe when no other fruit was. Apples grew wild in the Caucasus—and in what is now Turkistan and Kazakhstan—where there were forests of quite tall trees that were nonetheless ancestors of our apple trees. People ate apples early and often; remains indicate that ten thousand years ago in Switzerland, in Great Britain, in the lakes region of

Italy, and probably in dozens of other places, people munched on them. We find evidence of apples in cultivation at Ur, in Egypt, and at Jericho by 6500 BCE, in China by 5000 BCE. Apples readily mutate and so varieties tasty and terrible are always being created. To avoid that, apples are usually grafted onto crabapple stock. People have also been eating crabapples for a long time. The Romans spread apples in thirty-seven varieties wherever they could; the poet Horace said that the perfect meal began with eggs and ended with apples. The Pilgrims brought apple stock with them when they came to America and Johnny Appleseed spread apples westward. We all know that apples are good for us, containing vitamin C, antioxidants, potassium, folic acid, lots of fiber, and calcium.

Walnuts are common in Ashkenazi Charoset. People have been eating walnuts for thousands of years since they grew wild from eastern Europe through Asia Minor to the Himalayas, and in different species all through the Americas. The Persian walnut is the common one in commerce. The Carpathian walnut is just the hardier northern version of the Persian. The native ones here in the States are black walnuts, the ones that are murder to crack and stain your hands and anything else they touch. The earliest proof of people eating walnuts has been found in a cave in what's now Iraq and one in Switzerland. One thing I know about the tree is that you can't plant it near a garden—its roots will excrete a toxin that kills other plants. It is a jealous tree.

I never make the kind of Charoset described above. Because I cannot digest true nuts like walnuts (or hickory nuts or brazil nuts), I make a Sephardic Charoset every year.

Sephardic Charoset #1

Chop whole unsalted almonds in the food processor or by hand until they are in small pieces, but do not make almond butter out of them.

Add a bit of whole cinnamon—we are really talking cassia here, of course.

Add dates—I prefer deglet noor and I pit them. The
   already pitted dates are sometimes dry.
Add apples, cored but not peeled.
Add some dried figs,
some ground cinnamon,
some ground allspice, less than the cinnamon.

I don't soak the dried fruit first for this recipe, but just cut it into the apples.

Chop into small (but not too small) pieces and put in a bowl with sweet kosher wine. I save a little out at this point to mix with grape juice. There are always one or two ex-drinkers at our seders who cannot touch wine. I keep their Charoset alcohol-free.

You can alter the above recipe in many ways. When you chop cinnamon sticks with the almonds, you can also put in some fresh ginger—not too much.

Some recipes add honey. For me, it's quite sweet enough
with the figs and the apples and the sweet wine. But if
your kids like it super sweet, add honey to the fruit when
you are chopping it.

◎

Sephardic Charoset #2

Almonds again and dates and apples, but oranges get
added and a bit of orange juice and orange zest. Ginger
always accompanies the cinnamon in this version. This is
a Sephardic Charoset originating in Spain.

◎

Mizraki Charoset

Almonds and pistachios chopped together
Dates
Raisins
Figs
Sesame seeds
Apples
Pomegranate seeds
Pepper
Ground ginger
Cinnamon
Ground cardamom
Whole cloves in tiny pieces

Chop together and taste.

◎

There is no correct Charoset. Wherever Jews lived, they created hundreds of regional variations. Charoset is loose that way, the item on the seder plate that exists to please you. We pretend it suggests mortar but it doesn't really. That's an excuse, and we all know it. Jews have acknowledged that little fib by creating Charoset that indulges the local appetite and incorporates whatever would be available at that time of year, including in their recipes coconut, chestnuts or chestnut paste, dried apricots, cherry or orange brandy, hazelnuts, pecans, dried pears, sesame seeds, wine vinegar, green chili peppers, tamarind juice, candied fruit, lime juice, watermelon, bananas, avocados, and pecans. You get the idea: some kind of nut, one or various fruits, spices and sweet wine or grape juice. Be creative, but not too. I have a friend who never uses recipes but takes pride in her originality. Her meals are usually edible but seldom enjoyable. If you want to invent something, try a small amount first.

Notice that in none of these recipes except the first are there exact ingredients listed. There are two reasons: I don't know if you are doing a seder for two or for twenty. If you make a lot and have some left over, just refrigerate and enjoy. It keeps well. If you are having a second night seder, you have two choices: make a different Charoset for each night, or make enough the first night to suffice for the second. The last reason for not giving exact measurements is that apples, if you are using them, vary incredibly in sweetness or tartness. How much sweet wine or sugar or honey you need is best left to your taste buds. Chop, mix, taste. Then chop some more, mix some more, taste some more. When I am making Charoset, I am always correcting the balance with more of this to offset too much of that. Play it by tongue and texture.

One reason I like the Sephardic and Mizraki recipes is that they often contain figs or dates, both of which go way back as foods—figs are referred to in Sumerian tablets and were known five thousand years ago in Arabia and soon after in Egypt—and beyond being referred to in the *Tanakh* numerous times, are still important and popular foods in the Middle East. Figs belong to the mulberry family. Remember the fig leaves in the Garden of Eden? Besides, they're good for you—extremely high in fiber, full of calcium, iron, phosphorous, and potassium. Buddha had his revelation under a fig tree. They like it warm and arid.

Dates grow on a palm tree believed to have originated around the Persian Gulf. They seem to have been in cultivation in Arabia for six thousand years at least, and at Ur in what's now Iraq for five thousand, but remains indicate they were eaten far earlier than that. Since dates do not readily decay and are high in food value, they were a popular food for caravans. Thus were date palms planted in oases across the Middle East, Arabia, Egypt, the Sahara—in deserts—wherever people nibbling on dates dropped the pits. It likes a long hot dry summer and abhors humidity. It's a stately and attractive tree; Tamar (Hebrew for "date palm") and Tamara are still popular Hebrew names for girls. Dates are rich in fiber, sugar, several B vitamins, vitamin C, and many minerals including potassium. Dates were used to sweeten wine and to make date wine, which must have been paralyzingly sweet. I've read that it is still made and drunk in rural Egypt. Dates were reputed to be an aphrodisiac—but after reading that about horseradish, I remain unconvinced by any of these foodstuffs.

Almonds are thought to have originated in China or Central

Asia and to have been brought back along the Silk Road. In the same way that the desert caravans ate dates en route, the caravans of the Silk Road ate almonds. But there are also claims that they originated in western Asia or in North Africa. They are related to peaches and plums. Almonds were grown in the Middle East and in Turkey quite early and were prized. In Genesis, Israel tells his sons, who have met with Joseph in Egypt without recognizing him, to take him gifts including almonds and pistachios. Remember that Aaron's rod turned into a blossoming almond bough, complete with nuts. The original menorah, the golden lamp stand, was decorated with almond blossoms; gold almond blossoms formed the holders for the oil that burned day and night. *Shakad*, Hebrew for "almond tree," implies haste, for almond trees were among the first to bloom in the spring. Almonds were thought from Roman times to prevent drunkenness. They were also considered in many societies (Roman and Swedish, for example) to be a symbol or a bringer of good fortune. They have been associated with weddings for centuries, often with a candy coating. This is all about the sweet almond; the bitter almond is poisonous.

I love recipes, even the ones I never make. I find the regional variations fascinating. Charoset is one part of Pesach where you can freely play with food. Some years I make more than one type. It's fun and it recalls to us the width, the diversity of our Diaspora and how many ways there are and have been to be a Jew.

Here is a Greek-flavored Charoset:

◎

Mix twice as many dried apricots, roughly cut into
quarters, into half as many sultanas—yellow raisins.

Add as many dates and as many figs as you have apricots,
and mix it all well.

You can soak the dried fruit overnight if you like.

Briefly sauté pine nuts in Pam or a little olive or sesame
oil until they are just light brown. Don't let them turn
dark brown.

Grind the pine nuts *very* briefly or chop them with a
mezzaluna.

Mix everything and add fresh lemon juice and sweet wine.

Add cinnamon and taste.

◎

Here's an Israeli Charoset:

◎

Peel, core, and chop apples.

Peel and chop the same quantity of bananas, ripe but not
too.

Add about the same quantity of dates, pitted and chopped.

Add about half the amount of pistachio nuts, shelled and then chopped, briefly. Add the juice and zest of lemon, the juice and zest of orange, cinnamon, and sweet kosher wine to taste. Then add matzoh meal until the Charoset is of the right thickness.

©

Curaçao was the first place in the New World where Jews settled, coming over in 1651 from the Netherlands. These were Spanish Jews who had fled previously to the Netherlands. Here is an adaptation of a recipe for Charoset from them

©

Curaçao Charoset

Pitted dates
Pitted prunes
Figs
Sultanas
Cashews
Lemon, left with the rind on and just cut in chunks and
    the seeds removed
Honey
Sweet red kosher wine

Chop everything together coarsely. Add the wine
and honey. Chop more. This is going to be made into
little balls, so it will be of finer texture than the other
Charosets. Use a food processor. Refrigerate for at
least 1 hour. Then roll it into balls and dust with
cinnamon.

If everything I have listed is too plain for you, go to
Marthastewart.com. She has a cooked Charoset that comes from
Joan Nathan's *Jewish Cooking in America* and is called "Joan's Seven
Fruit Haroset." I'm sure it tastes great. If you have lots of help and
time, it sounds fascinating. Joan Nathan's *The Jewish Holiday Kitchen*
has some very sophisticated Charosets you might fancy.

Generally by the time you reach that point in the haggadah
where you make the Hillel sandwich of matzoh, Maror, and
Charoset, you are hungry and the kids are starving. Charoset
helps tempers and moods until you finish up that part of the haggadah and put the meal on the table. It sweetens the mouth and
the mood, signaling to everybody at the table, Not long now.

If you have children, let them help you make the Charoset.
You can enlist other adults in its preparation, too. Since, unlike
baking a cake, the ingredients are whatever you want to use and
the proportions go according to taste, kids or friends can also
make suggestions and chop or grind ingredients. Making
Charoset should be fun, lending itself to group energy and activity. Tasting is mandated and it smells great. It can be an excellent
time while making Charoset to talk about Pesach to your chil-

dren and prepare them for the seder. The scent of Charoset should seep into our brains with memories of the holiday.

Why do we want something sweet? I guess it's genetic, programmed into us along with our distaste for what is bitter. We call those we love, sweet or sweetie or sweetheart. Honey, sugar, sweetie pie, honeybunch—what is sweet is what we want. So in the midst of the seder, after we have told the story of the Exodus and worked our way through the longest part of the haggadah, after bitterness and the flat dry taste of matzoh, the bread of flight, we come to sweetness and pleasure, something we never have to be coaxed to eat. I suspect it was added for the children, but who is ever too old for sweets? It reminds us that while we carry out this tradition to connect with our past, our ancestors, our Jewishness, with justice and oppression and freedom, we also do it because it is pleasurable. Be sure that you make it so for yourself and your companions at the table. Do not worry so much about what is correct that you turn Passover preparations and ritual into a chore. Make it wonderful for yourself. Make it delightful for your friends and/or family. Make it rich and moving. Don't get stuck remembering how Zeyde did it or how your friend who knows far more Hebrew than you do and has studied Talmud does it. What is "right" ultimately is what works for you and yours: what gives you all a vivid and memorable night of haggadah and food, wine and singing, remembering and retelling, discussing and being together.

Mixing the Charoset and the Maror—or Chazeret as some people do—reminds us that our lives are composed of the sweet and the bitter, and so is the world around us. Both elements, both life experiences coexist, sometimes at the same time, sometimes on different days or years or epochs of our lives. But every life has both. Jewish writing is noted for mixing the bitter and the sweet, just as the Hillel sandwich does. I always leave the Charoset on the table during the meal so that everybody can take more, and they do. They do.

15
Tapuz

𝒜n addition to the traditional seder plate in recent years is an orange. It should be bright orange, pretty, and unblemished. I like to use a blood orange, for reasons I will discuss later on. For years I have been placing the orange on the plate and giving the following commentary:

When women were beginning to be ordained as rabbis, Susannah Heschel was speaking at a synagogue in Florida. A man rose in anger. "A woman belongs on the *bimah* as much as an orange belongs on the seder plate!"

I have seen variations of that explanation in many haggadahs and books about Jewish holidays and customs, sometimes with the woman rabbi being in Israel. But it turns out the whole story is bunk. Here's the real story. It does involve Susannah Heschel, the Jewish feminist writer, editor, and scholar, but she wasn't on the *bimah*. Instead, in the early eighties, she was visiting Oberlin. A feminist haggadah used at a seder there put a crust of bread on the seder plate, as a sign of solidarity with Jewish lesbians, symbolizing the lack of a home in Judaism for lesbians—so that they feel as out of place as a crust of bread on the seder plate.

Susannah Heschel felt that there should be an acknowledgment of those excluded from traditional Judaism, but that the bread was a poor symbol, since it suggested that lesbians and gays were truly out of place in Judaism and a violation of it, like chametz on the seder plate. She decided to use an orange instead, to symbolize rather the inclusion of those who have been "left out" of traditional Judaism—women in general, lesbians and gay men. The orange is a symbol of the fruitfulness of Judaism when all of us are included and given a place. The need to spit out occasional seeds stands for the necessity to "spit out" prejudices.

The orange for many of us is a strong female symbol. The seeds symbolize the future in the same way that an egg does. The mature fruit carries within it the future: a tree contained in a seed. From small beginnings can come great marvels. We hold inside ourselves the potential for rebirth, for strong new openings. Pesach is very much a festival of rebirth, of beginning again, of leaving the old and going into the new. Since you want the symbolism of the seeds within the orange, it is better to use Valencias, which have a few seeds, or blood oranges, but to avoid navel oranges, which are seedless.

An orange: Tapuz

Round you are and bright as a newly risen moon.
You are sweet and acid, dessert and medicine.
You carry within your curves the future
of your kind, those pale seeds winking
from the sections, each an embryo tree.

Come into your own and shine,
where the only roundness was the almost
hidden plate bearing up the ritual items.
Be subject as well as object. Sing
in your orangeness of female strength.

Clash if you need to. Roll if you must.
Center the plate about your glow.
We are, we will be, we become: rabbis,
yes, cantors, shapers, prophets, creating
a new Judaism that is yours and ours.

The writer Anita Diamant links the juiciness of the orange to the vigor of Judaism and sees in its presence a reminder that Judaism changes and must change. We need to remember that Judaism is a living tradition, not a dead letter, and that every generation has something to add to the tradition. The cup for Eliyahu was added only about five hundred years ago. Children should, when they ask about the orange, be told that it is a new addition and that it symbolizes the desire to include Jews who were left out—lesbians, gays, and women—present perhaps but marginalized, pushed from leadership and denied a true sense of agency.

Previously only the plate itself suggested a female presence—even though the story of Pesach begins with female rebellion, the refusal of the midwives to kill the male babies; even though we were told by Rabbi Akiva in the Talmud that it was because of the righteousness of the women that Hashem redeemed the people.

There is a lot about birth and rebirth in Pesach. The slaves must exit the "narrow place" (Mitzrayim—Egypt). And the whole people must flee through the Sea of Reeds—images of amniotic fluid and the birth canal. We speak of the birth of a people. We speak of personal rebirth. We speak of remaking our society in ways that lead to a birth or rebirth of freedom and justice.

The strangeness to many Jews of an orange on the seder plate is in keeping with the night that is different from all other nights and the meal that is different from all other meals of the year. It can provoke questions, which is part of what the haggadah is trying to do: make you question and mull over and reexperience everything in the seder.

I like to use a blood orange because the "blood" symbolizes for me the pain that ostracism has caused gays and women, the sometimes literal blood that has been shed because of notions about who deserves to be included as a Jew and who does not, who is worthy and who is not, who can take full part in whatever rituals they choose to join and who is not permitted into the straight male club. Women have died and are dying today because they are women: because they do not have good prenatal care or good obstetric care and die in childbirth; because they become pregnant and do not want or cannot have a baby and have no access to affordable, safe, nearby abortions; because they walk down a street late at night or early in the morning; because someone breaks into their house or apartment or catches them in a parking lot or garage; because they try to leave an abusive relationship; because they do not want a relationship with a man who stalks them; because they have the misfortune of living in a war zone and die of bombs, bullets or grenades, of being raped to death—collateral damage. Gays and lesbians are attacked in the streets, on the Appalachian Trail, in rural Wyoming, in bars and restaurants, at private parties. They are ostracized in school and on the job. In some states, they are denied the right to adopt children; in most states they cannot have legal partnerships and marriages, share health benefits, or make end-of-life decisions for each other.

On a night devoted to liberation and escape from oppression, it is tremendously fitting that we should have an object on the seder plate reminding us not to oppress those we may regard as other and to ask ourselves why we regard them as other. It reminds us to fight for all our full participation in Judaism and not to accept any exclusion.

Oranges probably originated—nothing seems to be known for sure—in Southeast Asia at least six thousand years ago. Early on the orange was brought to North Africa. From there it made its way into the Roman Empire. It seems to have been at home in southern Europe during the Middle Ages. Columbus brought seeds to the New World on his second voyage. All citrus fruits belong to the same genus but there are many species, and many varieties within each species. They seem to mutate fairly easily on their own and produce all kinds of variations—the navel orange was a mutation that appeared in an orchard in Brazil in 1820. I have seen statements that the first sweet orange was grown in Spain, where you can also find bitter oranges that are great for marmalade. Oranges are technically berries; the orange tree itself is beautiful, with sweetly scented white blossoms and glossy evergreen leaves. Several times on visits to California, I have slept in rooms where the soothing scent of orange blossoms wafted in.

That oranges have been around for a long time in India is

attested to by the origins of the word: from the Sanskrit *narangah,* orange tree, influenced by the Persian *narang,* into Spanish *naranja,* into Old French *orenge.* The fruit came first; the color derives its name from the fruit. Its beauty, its health-giving qualities, and its inclination to create new varieties makes it particularly suited to its meaning in the seder. If you want to divide up the orange and give a segment to each participant after the Hillel sandwich, that can be a pleasant reminder of our attempt nowadays to celebrate our diversity instead of denying it; our determination to give every Jew a voice and a hand in re-creating Judaism now and moving into the future. I think everybody would appreciate a section of orange at this point in the seder, when people are hungry and beginning to anticipate the meal. You may need to have a second orange in waiting to make sure everyone gets a piece, if there are more people than there are sections.

Therefore, for its rich and never more pertinent symbolism, I urge you to place an orange on your seder plate.

16
Beytzah: The Egg

Whoever heard of roasted egg before the seder demanded it? We scramble, we boil hard or soft, we poach and make omelets flat and puffy, frittatas, coddled eggs, eggs Florentine and soufflés. But roasted? It's easy enough to do if you have a gas stove or a grill or a hibachi or even a fireplace. You hard-boil an egg, cool it, remove the shell. Then hold the egg over an open flame on a long fork or shish kabob skewer. If you have a much better equipped kitchen than mine, you can use one of those little propane torches sold for crusting crème brûlée. After both seders are done, I always eat the egg. I like the strange taste and texture, but nobody else seems to. The egg is said to represent the *chagigah* sacrifice, an additional temple sacrifice traditionally offered on holidays.

In the case of the seder, which came first is easy to say. The egg comes first, and in many seders you never get to the chicken. Why an egg? We have that symbol in common with most societies—maybe not the Eskimo or the Laplanders. But most people live around birds and birds lay eggs and from the eggs hatch more birds. It all happens quickly enough for everybody to notice. So the egg is a common and handy symbol of birth, of rebirth in the sense of the continuation of a line, of fertility itself. It is curved like the sun and the moon, rounded like a woman's belly and breasts. A pregnant woman is more of an oblong than a circle, again the egg. I mentioned the sun, but eggs seem to me to belong far more to the moon, always full as it hangs over the seder. I compare the egg to the moon, yet like most New Englanders, I am prejudiced against white eggs. All the eggs I buy are brown. However, once peeled, brown eggs are as moonlike as white.

Eggs are part of the creation myths of many peoples. The Egyptians thought the world came from an egg. *Ab ovo*, we say, meaning "at the beginning." A course of eggs begins the feast at the center of the seder. The association of eggs and moon and female is obvious. We wax and wane, as does the moon, and our cycle in our fertile years is a moon-thly one. Out of the egg comes not only the bird and the lizard but the child.

The egg is also, of course, associated with spring. Modern chickens may lay year-round, but most birds lay their eggs in spring. Spring is an ancient new year's, and scholars believe that the Jewish year originally began with a spring festival. In the fall, at what is now Rosh Hashanah, we examine ourselves critically in the Days of Awe, asking ourselves what about us we want to discard, what we have done that has injured others to whom we must make amends, and we remember and mourn our dead. But in spring we are dealing with renewal and separation. All birth is a separation. Life is cyclical. There is an old Ashkenazi tradition of eating eggs while mourning, often at the first meal after a burial. Why eggs? Because life goes on and the lives of the mourners after sitting shivah must continue as they return to the rhythms and demands of daily life and work.

The egg contains within it potentiality—what will be. In its inner formlessness, form lurks. It is an immensely rich symbol that you can eat for breakfast. It urges us to ask of ourselves what lurks within that we have not yet brought out into the world. What so far inchoate dreams and intentions swirl inside our brains? Out of sticky fluid the process of growth brings forth bones and beak, wings and feet. What changes are waiting to sprout wings? Changes in ourselves, changes we want to make in the world? The egg cannot remain as it is, a pseudostone. It develops until the creature within breaks out, or it rots. The stench of rotten eggs is familiar and disgusting. An egg talks of intention even as it lies there, seemingly inert. Therefore, in order to act, we egg each other on. *Kavanah*, intention, is important, but less than a sigh if it does not lead to action. We may fail, but we are nothing until we try.

Beytzah

It's the season of the egg,
older than any named creed:
that perfect shape that signs
a pregnant woman, the moon

slightly compressed, as if
a great serpent held it
in its opened mouth
to carry or eat it.

Eggs smell funky
slipped from under
the hen's breast, hotter
than our blood.

Christians paint them,
we roast them. The only
time in the whirling year
I ever eat roasted egg:

a campfire flavor, bit
burnt, reeking of haste
like the matzoh there was no
time to let rise.

We like our eggs honest,
brown. Outside my window
the chickadees choose partners
to lay tiny round eggs.

The egg of the world cracks
open with spring and the wet
scraggly chick of northern
spring emerges gaunt, dripping.

Soon it will preen its green
feathers, soon it will grow
fat and strong, its wings
blue and blinding.

*Tonight we dip the egg in salt
water like bowls of tears.
Eliyahu comes with the fierce
early spring bringing prophecy*

*that cracks open the head
swollen with importance.
Every day there is more work
to do and stronger light.*

The fragility of the egg is part of what we notice most. It drops warm from the hen's body and she chortles, giving a cackle of satisfaction. *Look what I've done!* Eggs are easy to break, like intentions, like promises. We can't make an omelet without breaking eggs, we are told. Once broken, it's use it or toss it. Eggs have a built-in expiration date like so much of what we must do but so often don't. I don't know why we roast an egg on Pesach. Like matzoh, it speaks of haste. Or perhaps, like the shank bone, it stands for the once-sacrificial lamb, which was surely roasted. It's a funny replacement, an egg for a lamb. Cheaper, certainly.

I can think of no eggs in the Tanakh. Yet the egg is an ancient symbol. From eggs in mythology and reality, many creatures hatch—hummingbirds, lizards, fish, dragons, platypuses, condors, Tyrannosaurus Rex. We were each once an egg in our mother's ovary. Thus we, too, come from an egg, like the chicken and like the chickadee outside the window at the feeder, keeping alive.

It is traditional at the seder to have a basket of hard-boiled eggs, usually peeled, to pass and dip in salt water, but instead, I start the meal with a Sephardic egg dish. My own background is Ashkenazi, but I like Sephardic and Mizraki cooking. It is often healthier than my own tradition. I mix them.

◎

Passover Egg Salad

This works for fifteen to sixteen people, which is what we have every year. You can cut it in half or quarter it or double it.

4 medium cucumbers or 3 really long ones. Peel and slice into a big pretty bowl. You can get fancy with the slices if you like.
3 bulb fennels. Use the tender white part. When you are slicing and it begins to resist you, stop.
10 hard-boiled eggs

Slice the eggs and mix the slices of cucumber and fennel together with them. Then you want to dress the salad:

Salt
Good virgin olive oil to taste
Juice of 1 ½ lemons

This is kind of a joke, as some lemons are very juicy and some are miserly with their juice. So just juice half a lemon at a time, stir into the oil mixture, and taste. Add lemon juice until you can taste it, but it should never overwhelm the olive oil. Pour over the salad.

Before you boil the eggs, if you prick them with a pin or whatever, they will not tend to break and spill their innards untidily into the pan. If you run the boiled eggs under cold water for a couple of minutes, then as fast as you can peel them, it is a lot easier. The shells are cool and the eggs are still hot. That makes for quick, neat peeling. Much less frustrating than if you let the eggs cool completely and then try to pick the shells off.

◎

This egg salad can sit happily in its dressing while the first part, the longest part, of the haggadah is being read and discussed. Right after the Hillel sandwich (Charoset, Maror, and matzoh), this is what I serve.

It is an admirable start to the meal. It fulfils the egg and salt requirement and is delicious. Unlike most salads, it is still good the next day, if you have any left over.

So as the egg begins the bird, the egg begins our Pesach meal.

17
Gefilte Fish

*G*efilte fish is commonly served after the egg or egg course in
Ashkenazi usage. Once upon a time, gefilte fish was, as the
name suggests, a stuffed fish. Ashkenazi history is thick with fish,
because the kinds we ate were cheaper than meat. The most common fish eaten in the ghetto was salted herring. It is believed that
there would have been far more famine in Europe if it were not
for salt cod and salt herring. People ate a lot of salt then, as now.
I remember eating herring in various forms in my childhood,
some of which, like herring in cream and pickled herring, are still
available. It was one of two ocean fish we ate, being on the Great
Lakes. We ate fish generally only when my father caught them;
but I remember the salty herring. The other ocean fish we knew
well was salt cod, sold in boxes by fishmongers or in butcher
shops. It requires a careful desalinating process in the kitchen—
too little soaking and the cod is woody, inedible; too much soaking and it will fall apart and become rather disgusting.

On Shabbat, gefilte fish is still popular. It was originally made
by mincing or chopping freshwater fish, deboning it in the

process. The fish most commonly used for gefilte fish was carp, a very bony fish. Getting rid of the bones made it far easier and less dangerous to eat—a fish bone in the throat is trouble. Also mincing the fish and mixing it with breadcrumbs, matzoh meal on Passover, maybe ground nuts like almonds, maybe some minced vegetables like carrots or onions, and finally binding it with eggs made the original fish go much further to feed the whole family. Then the mixture would be packed back into the fish skin, closed with skewers or sewn shut, and boiled, simmered, or baked.

Nowadays we just use a poached fish deboned and minced fine. We make balls of it. We? I have fond memories of a carp swimming in my grandma's bathtub. She made wonderful gefilte fish. Thus when my havurah, which always held a second night seder for the Jewish community on the outer Cape, decided one April that we on the board were all going to make enough to feed everyone homemade gefilte fish, I was delighted.

All I can say is that it took us the better part of a day and when we finished, the house reeked. The process was so disgusting that although everybody who tasted it said our gefilte fish was great, I could not bring myself to eat any, nor could Ira. I am providing a recipe with many variations and suggestions, followed by other recipes. Just don't ask me to help. I have no idea why when my grandma made gefilte fish, her apartment didn't smell like the dump on a bad day, but her secret is lost forever. Obviously a lot of people make it with less trouble, but I won't pretend to expertise I don't have. I leave the gefilte fish manufacturing to mothers and Maneischewitz, unless a guest volunteers.

You start off with one or more kinds of usually freshwater fish: possible combinations are yellow pike and whitefish; carp or carp mixed with pike and/or whitefish; carp with tilapia. Whitefish is a confusing name. European freshwater whitefish are simply a type of carp. There are also North American freshwater whitefish, totally different, and Atlantic white fish, again something else. Whatever you find and decide to use, get the fishmonger to cut off and save the heads. If he will grind the fish for you, you're halfway home. If so, ask for the bones or what they call the rack—the backbone and smaller bones leading off it. You want this for the broth.

You take the fish heads (I confess this part made me a little squeamish when we were making our ill-fated gefilte) and bones and put them in a stock pot or other heavy commodious pot. Add some nicely sliced carrots— 5 pounds of fish, then add 2 or 3 carrots and 2 or 3 sliced onions and 2 sticks of celery, chopped. Add enough water to cover everything, add salt and pepper, turn on the heat, and bring it to a boil. Leave it on a high simmer for an hour. Remove the heads and bones and save the liquid. Put aside the vegetables cooked in the broth.

In the meantime, take your 5 pounds of fish. If the fishmonger wasn't enough of a mensch to mince it for you, you have to do it yourself. You can mince by hand, using a mezzaluna in a wooden bowl, or just do it in your food processor, but don't reduce it to a puree. Just keep hitting the pulse button as you would for onions, not to turn it to glop. The trick is to get the bones out and not include them in the minced fish.

Sauté 2 more finely chopped onions in olive oil until wilted but not browned. Add to the fish. Some people add chopped carrots. You want to add eggs—say, 4 if you are working with five pounds of fish. Some people hard-boil the eggs and chop them in. Some people add raw egg. Some add a combination. There is no one way to make gefilte fish.

Polish style adds sugar, quite a lot. Russian style does not, but rather uses pepper. Like just about everyone, I like the way I had it as a child, so I go for the pepper. At this point, get your liquid boiling again in that big pot. You form a little of the mixture experimentally into balls, feeling it to judge consistency. Then add enough matzoh meal for the balls to hold their shape. Don't put too much in right away. Some people add ground almonds at this point. Now form a ball experimentally to see if it needs more matzoh meal. You don't want it to fall apart, but you don't want it to form into a hard golf ball either. You want gefilte fish that holds it shape without being too stiff. When you are satisfied with the consistency, roll your balls between your palms. Drop them into the boiling stock, turn the heat to high, simmer, and put the lid on. You'll have to check the temperature from time to time to make sure it isn't furiously boiling or on too slow a fire. You're going to let them cook for about 2 hours. At that point, fish out a ball and check it. It won't taste the same hot as it will cold, but you can tell if it's cooked enough. If not, continue cooking.

Over the years, people have used dill or parsley in the balls or paprika, either mild or hot. In any event, when the balls are thoroughly cooked, take them out of their broth and place them on a platter adorned with the vegetables from the original cooking of the stock. Add parsley or lettuce to the platter as you like. Cover with plastic wrap and refrigerate until it is completely chilled. In the meantime, take the broth and chill it, too. It should gel. You can serve that on the side—some people like it, some don't. Serve with horseradish.

◎

The fish heads remind me of going over to visit a friend in high school. Her family was Finnish—Finnish was the language of the household and I learned enough so that I still remember a couple of phrases. Her mother made a creamy fish-head soup, which tasted fine but creeped me out when the fish heads floated to the surface and their eyes looked into mine. We have become a squeamish people. Formerly we ate every bit of every animal killed to feed us. Some of us still remember soup made of chicken feet. My reaction to making gefilte fish does not make me proud. In the meantime, here are some recipes that sound doable, if you like. Few modern recipes seem to use carp, but carp was the basic ingredient in most European gefilte fishes.

Carp are freshwater fish that probably originated in the Orient and in prehistoric times made their way into the Volga River and the Caspian and Black seas on their own initiative. After that, the Romans introduced them into the Danube. In Europe, they fit into the ecology as bottom feeders in rivers and lakes. They can occupy any water, from a rushing clean mountain brook to an almost stagnant and heavily polluted river or pond. They have been raised for centuries, perhaps millennia, in artificial ponds. The Egyptians did it, the Romans did it, even monks did it. The wealthier class in Western Europe and Germany liked to raise their own freshwater fish on their estates.

Goldfish are closely related to carp, and those gorgeous koi fish of Japan are simply selected and carefully bred carp. In the United States, carp are generally regarded as a nuisance fish apt to take over and drive out native fish. In Great Britain and other Western European countries, they're viewed as a sportsman's fish: they can get very large—up to seventy, even eighty pounds, and can live for decades. They have excellent hearing and scent and taste organs, enabling them to find their food in murky or muddy waters. They're smart and cagey. One famous British carp, Clarissa, is known to be at least fifty years old. My bubbah would not let me name her bathtub carp.

But Americans seem to disdain carp in favor of other freshwater fish, as you'll note in most of these recipes. I'll start with a vegetarian gefilte fish, an oxymoron but an appetizer that can begin your meal. (There are others in chapter 19, "The Feast.")

◎

Vegetarian Gefilte

2 large onions, chopped
12 eggs—10 hard-boiled, 2 raw
2 tablespoons olive oil
2 carrots, peeled and cut into rounds
2 good-sized boiling potatoes
4 teaspoons matzoh meal
Salt and pepper

Sauté the onions until golden brown. Puree the 10 hard-boiled eggs with two-thirds of the cooked onions. Put the rest of the cooked onions in a pot with 2 cups of water and bring to a boil.

Add the carrots to the onions in the water and cook for 30 minutes. Peel the potatoes and grate them or process them briefly in a food processor with a grating blade.

Add the grated potatoes, matzoh meal, the uncooked eggs, salt and pepper to taste to the pureed egg-onion mixture and stir well.

With moist hands, form 12 to 16 balls. Add them to the pot with the onion and carrot in it, and cook for 20 to 25 minutes over low heat.

Serve cold.

Gefilte Fish #1

FISH MIXTURE:
7 pounds carp, save bones
2 pounds pike, save bones
6 large eggs, beaten
1 large onion, minced
¾ teaspoon salt
¾ teaspoon sugar
¼ teaspoon pepper
½ cup water
¼ cup to ½ cup matzoh meal

2 carrots, diced
2 stalks celery, chopped
3 onions, sliced

Grind the fish together or use a food processor. Combine with eggs, minced onion, and seasonings. Place dollops into boiling water for 5 minutes. (This is a taste tester; add extra seasoning if desired.)

Line the bottom of a pot with the fish bones, carrots, celery, and sliced onions. Fill the pot half full of water and bring to a boil. Make fish patties and place in the boiling water. Turn down the flame. Cook 3 hours, covered. Add additional seasoning to the water, if needed.

Serves 18 to 20.

◎

Gefilte Fish #2

5 pounds fish (carp, tilapia, and any other fatty fish)
1 onion for the broth, plus 5 onions
2 carrots
1 celery rib
Salt and pepper
Peppercorns
Oil for sauteeing onions
2 hard-boiled eggs
2 eggs, beaten
Some dill weed, fresh or dried
Some dill seeds
Pinch nutmeg
Matzoh meal

Have the fish filleted but save the heads, bones, and skin.
Place bones, head, skin, 1 onion (for the broth), 1 carrot,
and the celery rib in a pot with plenty of water along
with salt and peppercorns. Bring to a boil and simmer for
1 ½ hours.

Cook 2 onions in oil until wilted. Place the fish fillets,
3 raw onions, 2 cooked onions, hard-boiled eggs, raw
eggs, salt, pepper, dill weed, dill seed, and a pinch of
nutmeg in a food processor and run the machine just
until the fish is ground but not mush. If it is too thin,
add a little matzoh meal. Strain the broth and return it

to the stockpot. Make golf-sized balls. Drop them carefully into the simmering broth. Slice the remaining carrot and add to the broth. Simmer for 1½ hours. Transfer the fish to a dish and pour about 3 tablespoons of the stock on top. Decorate with the sliced carrots. Chill. The stock should gel.

◎

Gefilte Fish #3

8 pounds total of pike and white fish, or carp, ground
4 teaspoons salt
2 teaspoons freshly ground pepper
4 large onions: 2 sliced and 2 grated
3½ carrots, sliced
Finely minced parsley
6 eggs, beaten
½ cup ice water
⅓ cup matzoh meal

Into a very large pot, put bones and heads of fish, half the salt, half the pepper, 2(3) of the onions (sliced) and the carrots. Bring to a boil with enough water to cover.

Put the ground fish into a bowl and add remaining salt, pepper, and remaining onion (grated), parsley, eggs, ice water, and matzoh meal. Blend well.

Form into balls using ⅓ cup of the mixture for each ball.
Drop into the boiling water and simmer, covered, for
about 1 ½ hours. Strain the broth over the fish balls,
decorate with cooked carrot slices, and chill.

◎

Gefilte Fish #4

5 pounds firm-fleshed white fish
3 onions, sliced, plus 1 whole yellow onion cut roughly
    into pieces
Celery stalk, sliced
3 large carrots, sliced
Salt
Freshly ground pepper
4 eggs, beaten
2 tablespoons matzoh meal
¼ cup cold water
5 medium beets, sliced

Grind the fish. In a large kettle, add the heads, bones,
and trimmings of fish, 3 sliced onions, celery stalk,
2 carrots, water to cover, salt, and pepper. Bring to a
boil.

While this is simmering, in a food processor blend the
remaining onion and the eggs. Add the onion-egg
mixture to the ground fish, plus the matzoh meal, salt,

pepper, and some cold water, a little at a time, up to
¼ cup.

Strain the broth from the pot and discard the leavings.
Shape the fish mixture into balls. Layer beets on the
bottom of the pot. Add some sliced carrots, some onion
pieces, then fish balls. Repeat with everything but the
beets, end with some carrots. Pour the broth over the
fish. Simmer, covered, for 2 hours. Then strain the broth
and chill separately from the balls.

When cool, put fish balls on a plate and garnish with
sliced cooked carrots. Serve with the jellied fish broth—it
will be a beautiful scarlet—and horseradish. The fish
balls, however, do not turn red so long as you keep the
beets as a bottom layer.

Serves 18.

◎

Here is a way to cheat, conveniently.

◎

Tarting Up Bought Gefilte Fish

4 medium beets, peeled and with the ends cut off
5 carrots, peeled
2 large yellow onions

1 large jar gefilte fish, whatever kind you prefer
Freshly ground pepper
Salt to taste

Slice beets, carrots, and onions. Layer in a heavy pot all
the beets, some gefilte fish balls, some onion slices, some
carrots slices, and seasoning; repeat as many times as you
can, except for the beets, which only go on the bottom.
Pour the liquid from the jar over the fish and bring to a
boil. Turn down to a simmer and cover the pot. Simmer
for 45 minutes to 1 hour. Cool before serving.

Serves 6.

◎

So whether you buy your gefilte fish or make it yourself, that's
enough of that.

18
Chicken Soup

What is left to say about chicken soup that has not been said again and again? Yet this is a dish with which I have an intensely personal relationship going back to earliest childhood, a relationship undiminished by growing up and growing older.

I know at least sixty recipes for chicken sautéed, roasted, whatever, with many variations on each, but I generally make only three chicken soups. Both of the Ashkenazi ones are traditional and almost ritualized, although as I will explain, I cannot make chicken soup as my mother did, in one respect. The first of the two Ashkenazi soups is what I call the daily chicken soup to which, besides a whole chicken cut up or chicken parts, is added vegetables, a starch, onions, garlic, and always a little turmeric and dill, parsley and/or sometimes tarragon. A little white wine is spooned in to leach some calcium from the bones. You can use a whole chicken and serve four or five or two days' supper for two; or you can start with half a chicken or the equivalent in chicken parts and have just one night's supper for two or three. I have made chicken soup with whole chicken, with wings, with legs, and, when I was a poor graduate student, with backs and gizzards.

The other chicken soup is basically the accompaniment—the piano playing under the voice of a great tenor—to matzoh balls. It's a soup with little added, just the rich broth and the chicken, always a whole chicken. Some of it is set aside for the next day's meal. That is the Passover version of chicken soup, simple but perfect.

Chicken soup is just as good for you as Bubbeleh always said it was. One of the standard treatments for flu in our house is chicken soup and champagne. True *méthode champenoise* wine will often break a fever. Chicken soup is good for what ails you. Together they will make you less sick and certainly happier.

What I still miss from the chicken soup of my childhood are the unborn eggs. We were dealing with chickens that, when we met them, were still alive. We plucked. Then we took tweezers and carefully yanked out any stubs of feathers. Sometimes we cleaned off the feathers and tied them for dusters. This was work that my mother and I did at the kitchen table in the small busy kitchen of our tiny asbestos-shingled house, often to the accompaniment of whatever music we could find on the radio. Sometimes we sang. My mother had a sweet voice and liked to sing. We eviscerated the chicken. When we came to the eggs—often one with a shell but most of them shell-less little globules of yellow and sometimes red—we would tenderly lift them from the chicken to put aside. Later on in my childhood, we had a refrigerator and they would immediately go in there to wait for the soup to be almost done. Then gently we would stir in the unborn eggs for the last five or six minutes. When we were roasting a chicken, we would often pull out the fat and render it. I am more inclined to render goose fat these days, but sometimes I still render chicken fat. One side effect is one of the sweetest cooking aromas I know.

Many of the Jewish dishes I make are from my grandmother, who created the seders of my childhood, but daily chicken soup is something I learned from my mother. She was much more of a baker than a cook, but she created excellent soups—celery soup; potato soup; Scotch broth; tomato, beef, or lamb and cabbage borscht; mushroom and barley soup. She made an excellent turkey soup. Certainly she bought soups, especially those she and I had for our lunch, but soups for supper or dinner were always homemade. It was not that my grandma did not cook chicken soup, but that I never helped her, as I always did with my mother.

Grandma said that Jews always had chicken soup, because you may not have owned cows or sheep if you were very poor, but always there were chickens. As a child, she had fed them every day. In tenement yards, she had tried keeping them in Pittsburgh, but they would get stolen or something would go wrong. Chickens can be kept in a much smaller space than a cow, produce eggs that are pareve, eat just about anything, and reproduce as rapidly as you let them. As a side note, other soups my grandmother made, but not my mother: sour cherry soup, cold meatless borscht, and schav (sorrel)—all of which I also cook. You can, by the way, make schav from wild sorrel instead of garden sorrel, but I wouldn't recommend it. It takes a great heap of wild sorrel to make a little soup. It is one of those tasks I have done once and once only, like making ketchup from tomatoes and like creating bayberry candles. Life is too short unless you have recently retired without a plan and are in need of something truly taxing. With the ketchup, start with a bathtub full of tomatoes. After you have finished, hire somebody to scrape the ceiling over the stove. You will have two exquisite pints and a mess.

Darwin traced the origin of the chicken to something called the Red Jungle Fowl of Asia, and according to Margaret Visser (*Much Depends on Dinner*, Grove Press, 1999) domestication came late. Horses, dogs, cats, cattle, sheep, and goats all came to live with us long before the chicken was captured and tamed. As far as I can figure out from my reading, the Chinese seem to have been very early to domesticate chickens for eating—as opposed to cockfighting, use of their feathers for decoration or chicken divination. No ancient Hebrew sources deal with chickens. The Persian Empire seems to have spread chickens into Europe through Greece, but the Romans were unusual in eating them. Eating a chicken seems obvious to us—I grew up consuming chicken at least weekly. It was not, however, obvious to most who encountered the bird. They saw them as fighting, gaming animals.

Besides chicken soup, the other way my grandmother and my mother prepared chicken—not counting chopped liver, of course—was called roast chicken but was actually a pot roast. The chicken was cut up, usually, and then cooked, covered, in the oven with a little broth or wine, celery, onions, carrots, and the usual herbs. Half a cup of liquid is usually ample for a whole chicken. Potatoes might be added. My grandmother used garlic but my father hated it, forcing my mother to omit it, muttering about its absence every time. She was perfectly aware of the health benefits of garlic. My grandmother was full of herbal lore and domestic lore, such as the use of spiderwebs on wounds.

Chicken soup is one of the dishes that both Ira and I know how to make and make very well. But matzoh balls are one of his specialties.

◎

Daily Chicken Soup

This is not for Pesach.

1 chicken, cut up. You can also use chicken parts,
   especially if whoever you are cooking for, including
   yourself, has a strong preference for dark or light
   meat. You can also use gizzards and backs. You can
   use any kind of chicken, including roasting chickens,
   fryers, and old hens. The older and bigger the chicken,
   the longer it must cook.
1 tablespoon white wine or dry vermouth
Salt
3 carrots, sliced. All these vegetable quantities are totally
   arbitrary. Use more or less as you choose. I like a lot of
   carrots.
2 stalks celery, cut up in rounds; if it has leaves, chop them
1 big onion, roughly minced
2 cloves garlic, minced
1 or 2 parsnips, cut in rounds (optional)
Parsley, minced
Dill is good; tarragon always goes well with chicken;
   thyme is also good. You can add a bay leaf if you like.
   Cook's choice.
Some green vegetable, like green beans cut into thirds or
   kale, chopped (optional)
You may want to add noodles, spaetzele, kreplach,
   mandlen (those little dried dumpling pillows sold in

kosher grocery stores), rice, whatever. (I like to add
wild rice or whole wheat noodles)
Turmeric or saffron, to give a beautiful yellow color

Cut up the chicken, place in a heavy-duty soup pot, and
add around it 8 cups of water for a whole chicken. Add
the wine immediately. The alcohol will dissipate and you
will be leaching some of the calcium from the bones to
make the broth even more nutritious. Add some salt.
Some cooks throw in a chicken bouillon cube to make
the broth stronger. If you do that, go easy on the salt.
Maybe you want to go easy on the salt anyhow.

Add the vegetables but hold on to the herbs except for
thyme or bay leaf, if you are using them.

Bring to a boil and then turn down to a full simmer and
cover it. Essentially you're free to set the table and figure
out what else you want to add. If that includes rice, do it
around the 1-hour mark if you are using brown or wild.
Around the 1½-hour mark, if you are using white rice,
put it in and also add any green vegetables you may want
in the soup at that time.

At the hour and forty minute mark, add noodles or
kreplach. Add the other herbs, such as tarragon or dill, at
this time and the yellowing agent—turmeric or saffron.

Five minutes before serving, taste it—carefully. You
won't enjoy supper with a scalded tongue. See what it

needs. I expect, nothing. But your judgment comes into play again here.

If you had the unborn eggs, this would be the time to slip them into the soup.

This is a filling soup, not a first course.

◎

Ira Wood makes the Pesach chicken soup in our house and the matzoh balls. These are his recipes.

◎

Pesach Chicken Soup with Matzoh Balls

This is the purest chicken soup—its ingredients as simple as its preparation, basically a flavorful broth prepared to give emphasis to the matzoh balls.

5 quarts water
One 5- to 6-pound chicken
2 onions
2 stalks celery
2 carrots
3 chicken bouillon cubes
1 tablespoon turmeric
½ cup fresh parsley
½ cup fresh dill
2 teaspoons salt (or more, to your taste)

Fill a 10-quart pot halfway full with water. Plop the chicken in whole. (Do *not* skin it.) Add the onions, celery, and carrots, roughly chopped. Bring to a rolling boil. Drop the heat to a low simmer. Add the turmeric, parsley, and dill. Cook as long as feasible, at least 2 hours. We try to start the soup in the morning, drop the flame to as low as the stove allows after the boil, and cook, simmering, for the better part of the day, usually until early afternoon.

Turn the heat off and let the soup cool. Lift the chicken out of the pot with a slotted spoon (it will be in parts). Drop the chicken in a bowl until it is cool enough to pull all the meat off the bones. Drop the meat (and skin, too, if you like) back into the soup.

@

Matzoh Balls

The following recipe is for ten medium-size matzoh balls. Double, triple, etc., for more. We usually quadruple the recipe. Our 10-quart pot holds 40 matzoh balls.

4 eggs
¼ cup goose fat (see Notes) or chicken fat
¼ cup chicken soup from the pot (or seltzer) (see Notes)
1 teaspoon salt
1 cup matzoh meal

Beat the eggs. Add the fat, the soup, and the salt. Mix well, add the matzoh meal, and stir thoroughly. Cover the bowl and refrigerate for at least 1 hour.

Bring the soup to a boil. Scoop about a tablespoon of the chilled mixture from the bowl, roll in the palm and then on a cutting board to form balls, about 1 inch in diameter. Drop the balls into the boiling soup, being careful of the backsplash.

When all the balls are in the soup, lower the heat to medium, and cook 30 to 45 minutes. Drop the temperature to a simmer.

When serving always ask how many balls the guest wants, place the balls in the bowl first, then ladle in soup. They'll ask for more.

NOTES: We have a goose every Thanksgiving, render the goose fat, and save it in the back of the refrigerator in a tightly covered mason jar. Substitute rendered turkey or chicken fat, or use vegetable oil.

The difference between the floater and the sinker is seltzer (or any carbonated water). Add carbonated water for light and fluffy; add chicken soup stock for solid and chewy.

If you make floaters (light and fluffy matzoh balls), as many of the balls as possible will bob on the surface.

Depending on the amount of balls you make, there may not be enough room for all to reach the top. This is okay. The others will be just as good.

◎

Tricks of the trade: A dear friend who has come to Pesach at our house every year for over twenty years has never invited us to his home. We like him and thought, Okay he doesn't cook. So what?

One day he called up in a panic. "I'm making matzoh balls for a dinner party and they're falling apart in the pot. What should I do?"

Woody patiently walked him through all the ingredients above, matzoh meal, eggs, fat, etc. "Guess you'll have to start again from scratch."

"So what did I do wrong?"

He dropped the balls into simmering, not boiling, water. And he didn't invite us, the schnorrer. *Always make sure the soup is boiling before you drop the balls in and they won't break apart.*

If you have leftover chicken, you can quickly make up something quite different.

◎

Mizraki Chicken Soup

Take the leftover chicken and first make up a broth from cubes (I use only the Israeli chicken cubes) or leftover stock—as from the previous soup. Add cooked rice or else cook rice in the soup. (Remember that in Sephardic and Mizraki traditions, rice is okay for Pesach.) If you are aiming for 4 servings, use ½ cup uncooked rice. When the rice is tender, beat 4 eggs thoroughly in a separate bowl. Add the juice of 2 or 3 lemons and beat. Lemons vary so much in their juiciness that I cannot be specific. You can always add more but you can't take it out once it's in.

Turn down the fire under the soup to low and take out 1 cup of liquid. Beat it a little at a time into the egg-lemon mixture. Then return it all to the pan and cook at very low heat. Add the chicken and simmer it—only a simmer: if you boil it, you destroy the texture.

◎

This is a light soup and a change from the heavier food of the seders. If you follow Ashkenazi rules for Pesach, you won't make this till after the seven or eight days. If you follow Sephardic or Mizraki rules, you only avoid the grains forbidden in Torah during Pesach: wheat in other forms than matzoh, oats, barley, rye, and spelt. Then this soup is just fine. Rice doesn't ferment like the forbidden grains, but it is often included in the chametz list with the grains that do, as well as corn and legumes in Ashkenazi usage. Malt, baking powder, and yeast are also not used. Fermented wine vinegar, cider vinegar, and wine vinegar are fine in everybody's usage.

◎

Sephardic Chicken Soup

This is a serious soup, not one made with leftovers. Again, it uses rice.

1 whole chicken (you may or may not want to remove
   the skin)
6 cups water
2 cups white wine
Bunch of Italian parsley
2 carrots
2 onions, quartered
Thyme
A little turmeric
1 teaspoon salt or less, as you like
½ to ¾ cup of rice
2 eggs
Juice of 2 lemons

Put a whole chicken, the liquids, parsley, carrots, onions,
thyme, turmeric, and salt in a large pot. Bring to a boil,
cover, and let simmer for 1 hour.

Remove the chicken and cut the meat from the carcass.

Add the rice to the broth and cook it until rice is tender,
about 15 to 20 minutes with processed white rice; more
if you are using brown rice.

Beat the eggs, slowly adding the juice of the 2 lemons.

Take 1 tablespoon of the hot soup and stir it into the egg-lemon mixture. Do this 1 tablespoon at a time until you have put in about 2 cups. Then you can slowly add the rest. Return the soup to the pot, put the chicken back in, and heat it on a low flame. Be careful not to curdle the eggs, but you want to cook them.

In non-Pesach usage, there is another Ashkenazi soup named the New Mother Soup, which is just rich chicken broth with noodles, cooked chicken, white wine, and then eggs beaten into it, which is close to but different from the Mizraki version. There are many chicken soups from the Middle East and from India that add ginger, various spices, tomatoes, and one with lamb and rice balls for Pesach.

The scent of chicken soup cooking on the stove permeates the whole house. Part of our sensual experience is smelling that redolent soup. Even if Ira is sick in bed, even if I am sick, even if I cannot stand the sight or smell of almost anything I would normally scarf down, chicken soup promises and delivers.

It's inescapably wed to my notion of Jewish identity, and while there may be an element of Borscht Belt humor to the association, there is nothing more elemental to me. I may or may not feel on a given evening like facing or cooking a piece of meat or a stir-fry or a casserole, but I can always eat and keep down chicken soup. The daily version is a meal in itself, with maybe some bread, maybe a salad, maybe nothing else at all. It's complete in itself and satisfying as something perfect in its kind must be.

That last thing I had better tell you is how to render chicken fat, if you wish to do so. I rather like rendering chicken fat or, once a year, goose fat. It's fun, if you don't mind cooking. If you hate to cook, you should just skip this.

◎

Rendering Chicken Fat or Goose Fat

You pull out or cut off all the fat you can and chop it into smallish pieces, but not too small. Then you put it in a small pan with a lid. Cover it with water, put the lid on, and turn it moderately high. Cook for about 25 minutes to reach the next stage. When it begins to make noises— sorts of popping and crackling noises—turn the heat down a bit and uncover it. Let the water cook out. Watch out for splatters. You will have some brown bits in it. Run it through cheesecloth or coffee filter paper. The brown pieces are cracklings. I like to salt them and eat them on a slice of rye bread or, during Pesach, on matzoh. The rendered fat goes into a mason jar (if it is still hot, put a silver knife in the jar so it doesn't crack). Pour carefully, as it can burn you badly if you're clumsy or too casual with the hot fat. When it has cooled a bit, put the lid on. You can refrigerate it for a considerable amount of time—4 months at least—and use it when you want. You can buy rendered chicken fat in kosher stores, but you have to render your own goose fat. I do, because nothing else is quite as good.

◎

Here is a recipe adapted from my friend Nicole Barchilon Frank for a good vegetarian soup you might want to make for an all-veggie Pesach.

◎

Potato Lemon Soup

This is enough to feed a decent crowd.

8 cups water or white wine, or a mixture
4 to 5 carrots
6 to 8 celery stalks
Head of garlic, minced or forced through a garlic
　　press
2 to 3 tablespoons virgin olive oil
10 medium potatoes, cut into thin slices or small
　　cubes
2 vegetable bouillon cubes (the Israeli cubes are good)
Juice of 3 or 4 lemons
½ teaspoon turmeric
Thyme, fresh or dried
Bay leaf, powdered
Pinch salt

Fill your soup pot two-thirds to three-fourths full of the liquid. Put on a moderate fire.

Grind up the carrots and celery in a food processor or run them through a food mill.

Add to the water, turn up the heat, and boil.

Skim the scum off the top.

Separately, sauté the garlic in the oil on low heat. Don't let it brown, but soften it. Add this to the soup and cook on a low flame for fifteen minutes, stirring occasionally. Add the potatoes and cook 20 to 30 minutes, until the potatoes are soft and can be mashed into the soup, which you should do. Add the bouillon cubes. Add the lemon juice, herbs, and spices. Stir and cook another 5 minutes or so.

◎

I have included several more vegetarian soups in chapter 19, "The Feast," as well as other vegetarian dishes suitable for Pesach.

19
The Feast

Remember that early on in the seder, we invite all those who are hungry or who are in need to come in and eat. To my mind, that includes others who lack their own seder to attend or who are needy in any sense—people who need a seder that is meaningful to them. After the lengthy first part of the seder and the eating of the Maror and matzoh and Charoset, the food is finally served. The scents of the feast are not to be dismissed as unimportant. Olfactory memory is strong. Certain scents evoke periods in our lives, events, holidays, relationships, trips abroad. The traditional foods of Passover need not be repeated every year, but you will want to continue to serve at least some of them because of their flavor and scent—often the whole house is redolent of Pesach cooking long before the cook shuts off the oven and sits down at the table to take part in the seder. Those aromas help to put us in the mood for Pesach.

Ira and I do all the basic cooking for the seder, but we ask people to bring various things: extra *matzot kosher l'Pesach;* gefilte fish, either in jars or, if they want to do it (as I have warned you, I never will again), homemade; kosher wines, sweet and dry. And often desserts. One couple always brings a green salad with the dressing in a bottle.

I serve a first course of the Sephardic Egg Salad (to be found in the chapter on eggs), but many seders begin with a simple hard-boiled egg dipped in salt water.

The egg course is generally followed by some kind of fish course. In Ashkenazi tradition, this is generally gefilte fish. See chapter 17 for suggestions and recipes. If you would like to do something different, here's a herring appetizer:

Chopped Herring

1 jar herring snacks in wine sauce
1 matzoh, rendered into crumbs
1 small onion, minced
1 well-flavored apple, peeled, cored, and cut into quarters
2 hard-boiled eggs
1 teaspoon sugar

Drain the wine sauce from the jar of herring into a small bowl. Crush the matzoh into it to absorb the liquid. Finely chop the herring, the onions from the jar, the minced fresh onion, and the apple. If using a food processor, pulse a few times. Add the soaked matzoh and hard-boiled eggs. Continue to chop until thoroughly blended. Season with sugar if you like, but taste it first. This will do for 4 or 5.

◎

If you don't worry about *kitniyot*, those little seeds (see page 23), then you could start with hummus or baba ganoush. They're always a great treat. Instead of pita bread, serve them with slices of cucumber or sweet peppers, or give people lettuce to scoop up the dip. Again, Ira said everybody knows how to make hummus; however, having been fed much bad hummus at parties, I give you the recipes I follow.

◎

Hummus

1 can chickpeas, drained
4 to 5 good-sized cloves garlic
½ cup sesame tahini
Juice of 2 lemons or more
1 tablespoon olive oil
1 teaspoon toasted sesame oil
Salt

I make it all in the food processor, starting with the chickpeas and garlic and tasting as I go. Often it needs more lemon. Then I spread it in a dish and mark the top with a pattern of olive oil with sumac powder sprinkled into the pattern. You can surround it with ripe black olives, preferably Calamatas. If you don't have sumac, you can use paprika. This makes enough for 6 or so.

Baba Ganoush

2 eggplants
4 to 6 good-size cloves garlic
½ cup sesame tahini
Juice of 3 lemons
1 teaspoon ground cumin
A little toasted sesame oil (optional)
Salt
Parsley or olives, for decoration

Preheat the oven to 425°F.

Prick the eggplant all over with an ice pick or a shish kabob skewer. (If you don't do this, you will be scraping eggplant off the roof of your oven.) Bake in the oven for 50 to 60 minutes, depending on the size of the eggplants. Then carefully skewer the eggplants so they do not fall apart and char them over an open flame. I have a gas stove, so it's easy. You could use a grill or a hibachi. Do not skip this step as it gives the proper smoky flavor to the dish. It's also easier to remove the skin from the eggplant if it's charred. When the eggplants have cooled just enough to handle, remove the skin in the sink.

Again, everything goes into the food processor. Freely adjust the lemon juice, tahini, and cumin as you go. You

can add a little toasted sesame oil. When you are
satisfied, put the mixture in the flat dish and decorate
with parsley or olives or anything you have on hand.

◎

If you don't want to follow the appetizer and/or fish course
with chicken soup, then perhaps you will like this Mizraki soup.

◎

Beef Soup for Pesach

1 tablespoon olive oil
1 pound chuck or brisket, cut into small cubes
2 onions, cut into smallish pieces
3 carrots, cut up
Tomato sauce, as you please
4 potatoes (such as Yukon Gold)
6 to 8 cups beef broth, water, red wine, or white wine
Fresh cilantro
2 or 3 large eggs
Matzoh, crumbled

Heat the olive oil over medium heat. Brown the beef in
the oil. Push it to one side or remove it from the pan
briefly. Sauté the onions. When they have just begun to
soften, add the carrot. Cook over medium heat for about
5 minutes. Then return the browned beef and add the
tomato sauce, potatoes, and your liquid. Simmer for an

hour or a little more. Brisket takes longer than chuck. Add the cilantro about 50 minutes into the cooking.

When everything is tender, beat 2 or 3 large eggs in a pan and then spoon the soup in, stirring. Turn off the fire and when you have added half the soup, then slowly pour everything back into the pot and stir well. Turn heat on again to simmer, and cook for 3 more minutes.

The matzoh can be crumbled into the soup before serving, or everyone may crumble their own matzoh into the soup.

Serves 6 to 8.

◎

Here's another hearty soup. I make this often in the winter and early spring. You have a lot of latitude with this soup. You can add more cabbage or potatoes, or less, or none. You can put in celery or leave it out. You can add parsley the last five minutes of cooking.

◎

Beef and Cabbage Borscht

3 quarts water, or part water and part red wine
2 pounds flanken, or any beef for stewing
6 beets, grated
2 onions, diced

2 cloves garlic, minced
1 mason jar or can of tomato paste or plum tomatoes
Salt and pepper to taste
About half a cabbage, red or green, shredded
1 tablespoon brown sugar
Lemon juice to taste
You can also add a potato or two, diced, or a bit of
    celery, diced

In a deep saucepan, combine the water and everything
but the cabbage, brown sugar, and lemon juice. Cover
and cook over medium heat for 1 ½ to 2 hours. Add the
rest of the ingredients. Cook 30 minutes longer. Taste
and adjust the seasoning.

Serves 8.

◎

Here's a vegetarian soup (I have another vegetarian leek soup
further on in this chapter).

◎

Leek and Mushroom Soup

FOR THE STOCK:
7 cups water or a little white wine mixed with the water
1 cup yellow onions, chopped
2 or 3 leeks, chopped, including the green tough parts

Handful of parsley
1 cup of celery, chopped
Bay leaf
Thyme

Combine all of these ingredients in a soup pot. Bring to a boil, then cover and simmer for 30 minutes. Strain out the vegetables before using, or mash them (except for the green part of the leeks).

Then start the rest of the soup.

4 or 5 leeks, well cleaned and sliced thin
2 tablespoons extra-virgin olive oil
2 turnips, peeled and cut into small cubes—you can use any white or purple and white turnip but I like the big winter Eastham turnips and need only one.
1 cup celery, chopped
1 bay leaf
Plum tomatoes
1 pound mushrooms—I like wood mushrooms, but use what you can that has some flavor.
Juice of 1 lemon
Handful of parsley, minced
Same amount of dill minced
Salt and pepper

Sauté the leeks and onions in the olive oil for 5 minutes over moderate heat. Add the turnips and celery and cook

for 5 minutes more. Then add the stock and bay leaf.
Bring to a boil, cover, and simmer for 15 minutes.

Add tomatoes and mushrooms and simmer for
15 minutes. Add the lemon juice and simmer 3 to
4 minutes more. Add the parsley and dill. Adjust the
seasoning.

◎

Stovetop Brisket

3 or 4 pounds beef brisket
4 carrots, peeled and quartered, then cut into pieces
   about 2 inches in length
2 stalks celery, leaves on, cut into slices
1 large onion, peeled and studded with 2 whole cloves
2 parsnips, peeled and quartered, sliced the same way as
   the carrots
1 bay leaf
3 cloves garlic, sliced
Handful of parsley, preferably Italian
Salt and pepper to taste
Cold water or red wine or a combination
1 *kosher l'Pesach* beef cube, to add more flavor if you like
Thyme
½ teaspoon allspice

Place the meat in a large pot with a lid. Add the carrots,
celery, onion studded with cloves, parsnips, bay leaf, and

spices. Cover with liquid and bring to a boil. After a few minutes of boiling, skim off the foam. Cover the pot, lower the heat, and simmer for 2½ hours or until the meat is fork tender. When the meat is cooked, remove from the heat and carefully remove the beef from the soup stock.

To serve, slice the beef and serve it hot or cold with horseradish, which you probably have on hand for the Maror, or with the vegetables strained from the broth. The brisket broth may be served separately as a soup course, with a portion of the cooked vegetables diced into it. Or you can cook it down, thicken it, and serve it as gravy. A little potato flour carefully stirred into some of the liquid and then added to the pot will work.

Remember that you can always use potatoes as a starch. Here is a hearty dish for vegetarians or a good side dish for the rest of us. I have served it with the stovetop brisket above, and they go well together.

Potato, Egg, and Onion Appetizer

3 or 4 potatoes
1 red bell pepper, chopped
1 red onion, grated or chopped fine in a food processor

4 hard-boiled eggs
2 tablespoons olive oil or chicken fat
Salt and freshly ground black pepper to taste

Boil the potatoes in their jackets until tender. In the
meantime, cook the pepper and onion together until
they are soft and well cooked. Chop the potatoes with
the eggs. Add the remaining ingredients and mix well.
This is a dish good served hot and just as good at room
temperature, which is an advantage on Pesach. If you
serve it unheated, you could arrange it on lettuce leaves,
thus having more Chazeret.

◎

Here's a good main dish, if you didn't serve chicken soup
already.

◎

Pot Roasted Chicken

Preheat the oven to 350°F.

You want to cut up a chicken for this usually, although
I remember that my mother didn't. If you use chicken
parts, brown them very briefly and remove to a bowl. I
use the same pot I will be cooking in. You can brown or
not brown the carrots, celery, onions, and garlic you are
adding. Then put the chicken back in. Add red or white

wine or stock or a mixture of both. You could also use cider. Add about 1 cup of liquid. If it gets dry during the cooking, add more.

Add herbs that you like with it: always tarragon and thyme, perhaps fresh parsley later on, sage, and bay leaf. It's up to you to season it as you like with salt and pepper.

Cover, bring to a boil on the stove, and then put it in the oven. After 45 minutes, add potatoes, cut small. I don't peel them, since I grow them. But many people do. Just cut them small enough. The potatoes can be omitted.

Cook for 1¾ to 2 hours, turning occasionally. Remember to add the potatoes 1 hour before you expect to be done.

All it needs to complete a good family dinner is a salad. If it's not Pesach, bread is nice for sopping up the juices.

◎

If you are making a vegetarian meal and did not serve soup after the egg, then Leek and Potato Soup or one of its variations is hearty and delicious, even as a main course.

◎

£eek and Potato Soup

Slice enough leeks to fill 4 cups (you could do up to one-third as yellow onions if you need to).

Slice enough potatoes to fill 5 cups. I do not peel them, although the original French recipes do.

Add 8 cups of water. Cover and cook until all is soft, around 1 hour. Don't let it stick or burn.

Grind up the soup using a food processor, or use one of those wands you can use to puree soup right in the pot.

If using a food processor, put the soup back in the pan and add milk, then some cream. I use skim milk and then, to finish, light cream. You can do any combination of milk—from whole to skim—and cream from half-and-half to heavy—that appeals to you and your constituency.

You may want to add Italian parsley or, after pureeing, some chives.

You can do endless variations on this basic soup: you can add celery when you put in the potatoes and leeks. You can add watercress toward the end, before you puree.

◎

Remember that at Pesach, you can adapt many recipes, such as Eggs Florentine (spinach, eggs, cheese, and cream done in the oven) for Pesach, staying vegetarian. Here are a pair of kugels that you might like, a traditional potato kugel and a less traditional one made with sweet potatoes.

◎

Sweet Potato Kugel

4 to 6 sweet potatoes, peeled (depending on size)
3 apples, cored
2 carrots
¼ cup brown sugar
1 cup dates, chopped
¼ cup matzoh meal
2 teaspoons cinnamon
½ teaspoon ground cloves
3 cardamom pods, or 1 teaspoon ground cardamom
1 cup chopped almonds
¼ cup orange juice
2 tablespoons olive oil

Preheat the oven to 375° F.

Grate the sweet potatoes, apples, and carrots by hand or pulse them until minced in a food processor. Place in a large bowl, add the remaining ingredients, and mix together. Pour into a 9 x 9-inch pan or a loaf pan and bake for 45 minutes, until the top is brown and crisp.

◎

Potato Kugel

6 potatoes
1 large, yellow onion
½ cup matzoh meal
2 eggs, beaten well
½ cup olive oil
½ teaspoon salt
Pepper to taste

Preheat the oven to 350°F.

Put the potatoes and onion through the coarsest grating blade of a food processor. Mix well with the remaining ingredients. Bake uncovered in an oiled 9-inch pan for 1 hour. The top should be golden brown. Taste from the middle to make sure the potatoes are soft and very well done.

Make sure to cook the potato mixture right away to keep the kugel from turning gray or black. Serve plain or with gravy.

If you'd like a side dish less heavy than the Tzimmes I described in chapter 11, "Matzoh," here's a nice Sephardic dish.

Carrots and Almonds

About 10 carrots, peeled and sliced—not too thick
2 tablespoons virgin olive oil
¼ cup fruit juice—orange, pomegranate, or apple
½ or more cups sliced almonds, briefly sautéed
1 tablespoon lemon juice
Chopped chives
Freshly ground nutmeg
Salt

Sauté the carrots in the olive oil for 12 to 15 minutes. Watch so they don't burn. Then add the fruit juice. It should be quickly absorbed by the carrots. Then stir in the almonds, lemon juice, chives, nutmeg, and salt. Cook, stirring, for another minute. This dish is very pretty.

Serves 10.

The following is a vegetarian Sephardic dish, but it uses ingredients common in Ashkenazi cooking, spinach and potatoes.

Spinach is often served for Pesach because it is a vegetable usually available fresh at that time of year in the northern countries.

◎

Spinach-Potato Casserole

6 to 8 baking potatoes, depending on size (If they are
   real lunkers, 6 will do.)
2 pounds fresh spinach, or 2 packages frozen, thawed
1 red onion or 6 shallots, minced
1 pound ricotta, low-fat or regular
Juice of 1 lemon
Salt and pepper to taste. If you are using a salty cheese,
   go easy on the salt.
8 matzot
2 cups grated cheese, your choice (mozzarella, cheddar,
   Monterey Jack, or a mixture)

Bake the potatoes before you start the recipe. Let them
cool well and then cut into slices.

If you are using fresh spinach, wash it, briefly cook it in
only the water still adhering to the leaves to wilt it, and
let it drain. Mix the spinach with the onions or shallots,
ricotta, the the lemon juice, and seasoning.

Soak the matzot in warm water for a couple of minutes.
Drain. Lightly oil a square-bottom pan and place a layer of
matzoh in the bottom. Add a layer of the spinach mixture,

then potatoes, then the grated cheese. Go on until you've used up your ingredients. Finish with a layer of matzoh.

Bake in a 350° oven for 30 minutes, until the top matzoh has colored to a deep yellow.

◎

DESSERTS

To be honest, after disastrous attempts to make potato-flour sponge cakes, I have given up. I followed the recipe faithfully. The cake rose beautifully. I took it from the oven, a fragrant and pretty cake. It stood there, trembled briefly, and fell in. I had a cake shaped like an extinct volcano. Now I get a cake from a kosher bakery in Brookline. My friend Elise brings chocolate-covered matzot. I love them, I confess, although they seem perverse—the opposite of what matzoh are supposed to signify. I would probably eat chocolate-covered cardboard if offered it.

Here is a dessert if you are serving vegetarian or dairy.

◎

Matzoh Custard

3½ cups matzoh farfel
Two 16-ounce cans sliced peaches, or the equivalent
    amount of frozen or fresh peaches
1 cup pitted dates, chopped

½ cup plus 2 tablespoons any kind of fat or oil you are
   comfortable with
8 large eggs
1 teaspoon whole nutmeg grated
½ cup plus 1 tablespoon dark brown sugar
One 8-ounce container plain yogurt, low-fat, no fat, or
   regular
One 8-ounce container cottage cheese, low-fat, no-fat,
   or regular
½ cup almonds or walnuts, chopped
1 teaspoon cinnamon

Preheat the oven to 350°F. Grease a 13 x 9-inch baking
dish or the equivalent.

Reserve ¼ cup farfel for the topping. In a large bowl,
combine the remaining farfel and 1½ cups warm water;
set aside.

Drain the peaches and cut each slice into 3 or 4 pieces.
Reserve ½ cup peaches and ¼ cup dates for the topping.

In a small saucepan over low heat melt ½ cup margarine,
or simply measure that amount of olive oil or fat you
prefer. In a bowl, beat the eggs, nutmeg, and ¼ cup
brown sugar, adding the yogurt, cottage cheese, and the
peaches and dates not reserved for the topping.

Fold in the soaked farfel, just until blended. Pour the
mixture into the baking dish. Sprinkle with reserved
peaches and dates.

For the topping, mix 2 tablespoons olive oil or
melted butter with the chopped nuts, cinnamon,
1 tablespoon brown sugar, and the reserved farfel.
Sprinkle the mixture evenly over the kugel. Bake 40 to
50 minutes, until the kugel is slightly puffed and set.

Serves 16.

◎

Here's a dessert that even I am not afraid to make for Passover.

◎

Passover Apple Sort of Crisp

⅓ cup almonds or walnuts
8 apples, cored and then chopped (I don't peel them)
10 large eggs, at or almost at room temperature
½ cup sugar
Juice and grated rind of 1 lemon
½ cup matzoh meal
Nutmeg and/or ginger to taste

Preheat the oven to 350°F.

Chop the almonds or walnuts in a food processor. Don't
make almond butter out of them. A light hand is necessary.

Then chop the apples, coarsely.

Separate the eggs and beat the egg yolks together. (A trick to separating eggs, if you don't already do this, is to break the eggs one at a time into 2 teacups. Then you transfer the egg white or yolk to a measuring cup and proceed to crack the next egg. That way, if you get yolk into the white, you can discard that egg and go on without screwing up your whole batch.) Add the sugar, lemon juice, and lemon zest. Stir into the apples. Add the matzoh meal, almonds or walnuts, and nutmeg and/or ginger.

Whip the egg whites until stiff enough to stand. Fold them into the mixture, pour into a pan, and bake for 35 to 40 minutes.

Serves 10.

◎

Here's another matzoh dairy dessert.

◎

Matzot with Cottage Cheese #2

4 matzot
Lukewarm water, or you can add a little white wine to
    the water
1 ½ pounds cottage cheese (I like small-curd low-fat
    cottage cheese, but you can use any kind)

½ cup raisins or sultanas
⅔ cup sugar, divided
1 teaspoon cinnamon
Butter for the pan (or oil or lowfat spray)
4 eggs, well beaten
2 cups milk
Juice and grated rind of 1 orange
¼ teaspoon salt

Preheat the oven to 375°F.

Soak the matzot one at a time in lukewarm water. Remove them carefully; press them gently between paper towels to remove excess moisture. Then combine the cottage cheese, raisins, ⅓ cup sugar, and cinnamon. Oil a 9-inch square baking pan. Place one soaked matzoh in the pan. Cover with a third of the cheese mixture. Continue layering, ending with the matzoh.

In a large mixing bowl, beat the eggs, milk, orange juice, orange rind, salt, and remaining ⅓ cup sugar until smooth and well blended. Pour the mixture over the matzot. Bake for 1 hour or until brown.

Serves 6 to 8.

◎

Here's the most traditional of all Pesach desserts, except maybe macaroons.

◎

Potato-Flour Sponge Cake

8 egg yolks
2 whole eggs
1¾ cups confectioners' sugar
2 teaspoons lemon juice
Grated rind of 2 lemons
Grated rind of 2 oranges
8 egg whites
⅞ cup sifted potato flour
⅛ teaspoon salt

Preheat the oven to 350°F.

Beat the egg yolks and whole eggs together. Gradually add the sugar, beating until thickened. Stir in the lemon juice and lemon and orange rind.

Beat the egg whites until stiff but not dry. Fold carefully into the sugar mixture.

Sift the potato flour and salt over it and fold in gently. Turn into a 10-inch tube pan. Bake for 45 minutes. Turn upside down and cool. Be very, very careful handling the cake as it can easily collapse. I have never succeeded in getting this cake to the table safely. You go ahead and try. I won't be fooled again!

Here's a variation:

8 eggs, separated
1 cup sugar
⅓ cup orange juice
Grated rind of 1 lemon
Grated rind of 1 orange
3 tablespoons potato flour
⅔ cup matzoh cake flour
A little salt

Preheat the oven to 325°F.

Using an electric mixer or food processor, beat the egg yolks. Add the sugar gradually. Add the orange juice and grated lemon and orange rinds.

Sift together the potato flour and the matzoh cake flour. Add to the mixture.

Beat the egg whites until they just begin to peak. Add salt and beat until stiff but not dry. Fold into the yolk mixture.

Bake in an ungreased 10-inch angel food pan for 1 hour. Turn the pan upside down, but let it cool completely before removing the cake. Cut very gingerly.

◎

I associate macaroons with Pesach, because they were what my grandmother always served. I don't think she baked them—she had plenty to do without that—but rather bought them in a kosher bakery in her Cleveland neighborhood. I used to buy macaroons, but I discovered that not everybody is crazy about them. If you would like to make them (I have done so, and aside from beating the egg whites, which I did in an electric mixer, it was not that difficult and I liked the results), here's a good recipe.

◎

Coconut Macaroons

6 egg whites, at room temperature
1 cup white sugar
4 cups of sweetened coconut flakes (I suggest dropping the coconut flakes in the food processor on a quick pulse to make the pieces smaller)
¼ cup chopped walnuts or almonds (I use almonds)
Matzoh cake meal

Preheat the oven to 350°F.

Beat the egg whites until they stand up. Toward the end, when they are thickening, add the sugar 1 tablespoon at a time without ceasing to whip the whites—easy in an electric mixer, but harder if you are beating by hand with a wire whisk. Add the coconut and the chopped nuts.

Drop the batter by the teaspoon on a greased cookie sheet, careful to make the macaroons approximately the same size. Let them stand for 15 minutes, then bake for 20 minutes.

Makes enough for 14.

◎

Almond Macaroons

2 eggs, separated
½ cup sugar
Pinch nutmeg if you like (not traditional but tasty)
1 teaspoon vanilla (get good vanilla; although it's pricey, it makes a difference)
2 cups almonds, ground in a food processor
Almonds, sliced or slivered, for decoration

Preheat the oven to 400°F.

Mix the egg yolks, sugar, nutmeg (optional), and vanilla. Fold in ground almonds. Set aside.

Beat the egg whites. Stop just when peaks begin to form. Fold the whites into the batter. Roll the batter into small balls, flatten slightly (a clean glass works well), and place on a greased baking sheet. Put an almond sliver or piece on top of each macaroon. Bake for 10 minutes, until the macaroons are lightly browned.

These keep superbly if stored correctly, so you can make these well in advance. I like them better than the coconut macaroons.

One variation is to add orange zest or orange peel when you fold in the ground almonds. You can also add a little almond extract with the vanilla. You could also decorate with a candied cherry or a sliver of candied orange peel.

◎

Dried Fruit Betty

This is an adaptation of a Sephardic dessert. It's pretty easy, even for me. I'm a great cook but a middling baker. My mother was the opposite.

1 cup dried apricots, well chopped
1 cup dates, pitted and well chopped
½ cup of raisins or sultanas
Enough sweet kosher for Passover wine to completely
    cover the dried fruit in a bowl
6 eggs
½ cup honey
1 ½ cups matzoh cake meal
1 ½ cups chopped almonds, walnuts, or hazelnuts
4 tablespoons virgin olive oil
2 teaspoons cinnamon
½ teaspoon ground ginger
Dash salt

Soak the dried fruits in the wine overnight. Drain off any not absorbed.

Preheat the oven to 350°F.

Beat the eggs well. Add the honey, matzoh meal, nuts, oil, spices, and salt and mix well.

Add the fruits, pour into a 9-inch square baking pan, and bake for 30 minutes. It should be still moist but spring back when you test it. Cut it into squares to serve. Makes 12 or 16 squares.

◎

Here's a kugel I consider a dessert.

◎

Pineapple Kugel

5 eggs, at room temperature
2 cups farfel
1 ½ cups orange juice, pineapple juice, or apple juice
1 ½ cups homemade or canned applesauce
1 can crushed pineapple in its own juices—the regular-size can, not the small one. If you use a small can, increase the amount of applesauce used.
1 teaspoon cinnamon
Grated nutmeg

¼ teaspoon salt
8 ounces butter or margarine or oil, depending on the meal
2 tablespoons white sugar
Additional cinnamon and sugar for sprinkling
3 tablespoons honey

Preheat the oven to 350°F.

Separate the eggs.

Soak the farfel in the juice, briefly. Then add the applesauce and crushed pineapple.

Beat the egg yolks with the cinnamon, nutmeg, and salt.

Add the oil or melted butter or margarine to the drained farfel. Then add the farfel to the yolk mixture.

Beat the egg whites until stiff. As you beat, slowly add 2 tablespoons sugar.

Fold them into the batter.

Spoon the batter into an oiled rectangular baking pan or a big pie pan. Sprinkle the top with a little cinnamon and sugar. Bake for 45 to 50 minutes.

It makes enough for 15.

This is a rather light feeling dessert, very tasty. You can add raisins if you like, to give it more texture.

◎

Here's a nice, easy dairy recipe.

◎

Passover Brownies

5 eggs, at room temperature
6 ounces bittersweet dark chocolate
¾ cup unsalted butter, softened
¾ cup sugar
1 teaspoon vanilla extract
A little salt
6 ounces ground almonds

Preheat the oven to 350°F.

Separate the eggs.

Melt the chocolate over a low flame or in a double boiler.

Mix the butter and sugar well. Add all the egg yolks. Stir in the chocolate, vanilla, salt, and the ground almonds.

Beat the egg whites until they're semi-stiff. Then fold into the batter.

Bake for 40 minutes. Cut into squares. This recipe does not make great brownies by conventional brownie standards, but everybody's had plenty to eat already. Its virtue is that it is chocolate and quick.

◎

This is a Sephardic dessert from Turkey, variously called Tishbishti, Tezpishti, or Tezpeshti. Whatever you call it, it's delicious.

◎

Tezpishti

SYRUP:
2 cups honey
2 cups water
Zest of lemon
1 tablespoon lemon juice

CAKE:
5 eggs
1 cup sugar
¼ cup olive oil
Juice and grated rind of 1 orange
2 teaspoons cinnamon
1¼ cup Passover matzoh cake meal
1¼ cup finely chopped almonds (but not too fine)

Preheat the oven to 350°F.

The syrup: Mix the honey and water together in a pan and bring to a boil. Add the lemon zest and lemon juice and simmer over low heat for 10 minutes. Cool.

The cake: Beat the eggs until frothy. Add the sugar and continue to beat until well mixed. Add the other cake ingredients, one at a time, stirring them into the batter. Pour into an oiled cake pan and bake for 30 minutes or until it tests done.

Remove the cake from the oven and pour the cooled syrup over it. Let stand for 2 hours, allowing the syrup to be absorbed. The honey causes it to stay fresh longer. Plenty for 12.

Collecting and trying and modifying various traditional Passover recipes has inspired me to try again, and this year I will make dessert for my seder instead of getting it from a kosher bakery. I have discovered I can do it. I have to say I really liked some of these desserts.

There are many wonderful recipes suitable for Passover that you can find in some excellent cookbooks. Joan Nathan's *Jewish Holiday Kitchen* has a number of Passover recipes. So does *Sephardic Cooking* by Copeland Marks, although it is not as easy to use, since the Pesach recipes are scattered throughout the cookbook, organized by country, whereas Nathan organizes by holiday.

After the meal is concluded and the afikomen shared out, then we always sing one of the contemporary thank-you's. The Birkat Ha-Mazon is recited or sung over the Third Cup of Wine, followed by a blessing for wine. Then you drink the third cup and launch into the second, shorter part of the haggadah. Remember, blessings are your opportunity to say whatever you feel is meaningful. In this case, you might want to express appreciation for the food and perhaps regret that so many people in the world don't get enough of it to sustain life or health. Or you might want to say something about how some of the ways that food is sold and processed and even some of the ways it is grown are actually decreasing our own health and despoiling the environment. Or maybe you just want to say how great the food was and how you appreciate the work that went into it.

20
Eliyahu's Cup

*E*liyahu gets a cup of his own at the seder table. It is either filled by the leader or—what we do—it is passed just before the Third Cup of Wine is drunk, and everybody puts a little of their wine into the cup, to signify what they will give up to make things better. We have two beautiful cups for Kiddush. At Pesach, one is the Kiddush cup and the other is Eliyahu's cup. Miriam, as you'll see in chapter 21, gets a clear wineglass at our seder, although some people also have a cup for her.

First the Fourth Cup of Wine is filled. Then the door is opened for Eliyahu. Perhaps historically this opening of the door was done earlier in the seder, when we invite in all who are hungry or in need to come in and be fed. But now the opening of the door is associated with Eliyahu.

Let's consider four new questions. Why Eliyahu? Why do we open the door? What is supposed to happen to the wine we put into Eliyahu's cup? Why is it appropriate to remember and to talk about the Holocaust right after Eliyahu?

Eliyahu was one of the most famous of the prophets. He was a man of great courage to do what he thought right, courage to confront those in power when he thought they were doing wrong. How is this prophet different from all other prophets? He appeared out of obscurity—he came from a rugged area in Transjordan—to challenge King Achav, king of the Ten Tribes, usually transliterated as Ahab. Ahab married a Sidonian princess, Izevel—transliterated commonly as Jezebel. She brought with her the worship of Ba'al to the tune of 450 priests and of Asherah to the tune of 400 priests, all supported by the treasury. As time went on, the priests of Hashem were persecuted and the religion of Ba'al and Asherah replaced Judaism. Actually, according to the most recent scholarship, she probably brought in Ba'al, but Asherah was worshipped beside Yahweh in ancient Israel and was not forbidden until much later.

Eliyahu confronted the king and demanded he return to the worship of Hashem. Ahab refused. Eliyahu cursed him and fled into the wilderness east of the Jordan to escape the king's anger. There he was fed by ravens. A great drought parched the land. After months, he was commanded to go into Sidon—heart of Ba'al worship—and hide with a particular widow. He performed miracles for her: he made her scanty supply of flour and oil miraculously replenish itself for the next two years and brought her son back to life.

Finally he marched back to the king to challenge the priests of Ba'al to a contest to prove whose deity was more powerful, more real. The priests of Ba'al danced around their altar while Eliyahu taunted them. Let their god burn the sacrifice if he could. Nothing happened. Finally Eliyahu rebuilt the old forsaken altar to Yahweh and slaughtered a sacrifice. He dug a trench around the new altar and had water poured over the altar and the sacrifice to prove there was no trickery involved. Then he prayed and Hashem burned up the water-soaked sacrifice and the altar.

The people responded by attacking the priests of Ba'al, killing them. Eliyahu then prayed and a great rain finally fell on the scorched land. Jezebel threatened to have Eliyahu killed the next day, so he fled into the wilderness. He seems to have been the equivalent of a mountain man—at home in wild places, perhaps even more comfortable there. He was one of the prophets who lived in caves, slept on the ground under a tree, and wore simple leather garb, eating off the land mostly—criticizing by their lifestyle the court and city habits they viewed as corrupt. It was very much a back-to-nature choice. The Eternal manifested this time as a still small voice—a whisper telling him he was not alone in his protests, that there were many others who were faithful. Eliyahu was sent to find Elisha, whom he took as his companion.

He told Ahab that dogs would lick his blood, his house would no longer rule, and dogs would eat Jezebel by the walls of the city. He appeared from time to time to rebuke Ahab, for instance after a murder for profit, and then to his successor, Ahaziah. The *Tanakh* says that he crossed the Jordan with Elisha, his spiritual heir, by smiting the waters. Then in Gilead he was taken up in a whirlwind in a chariot with horses of fire. Like Enoch, he was rewarded at the end of his natural life by a process of transformation so that he did not taste death.

The cup of Eliyahu

In life you had a temper.
Your sarcasm was a whetted knife.
Sometimes you shuddered with fear
but you made yourself act no matter
how few stood with you.
Open the door for Eliyahu
that he may come in.

Now you return to us
in rough times, out of smoke
and dust that swirls blinding us.
You come in vision, you come
in lightning on blackness.
Open the door for Eliyahu
that he may come in.

In every generation you return
speaking what few want to hear
words that burn us, that cut
us loose so we rise and go again
over the sharp rocks upward.
Open the door for Eliyahu
that he may come in.

You come as a wild man,
as a homeless sidewalk orator,
you come as a woman taking the bimah,

you come in prayer and song,
you come in a fierce rant.
Open the door for Eliyahu
that he may come in.

Prophecy is not a gift, but
sometimes a curse. Jonah
refusing. It is dangerous
to be right, to be righteous.
To stand against the wall of words.
Open the door for Eliyahu
that he may come in.

There are moments for each
of us when you summon, when
you call the whirlwind, when you
shake us like a rattle: Then we
too must become you and rise.
Open the door for Eliyahu
that we may come in,

for today we honor rebellion, those
who got up and left, not those
who stayed safe. For prophets
the times are always murderous.
The words they speak also burn them.
Open the door for Eliyahu
that he may come in, yet again.

In traditional Jewry, Eliyahu is expected to return three days or three years before the Messiah comes. Over the centuries, Eliyahu became a mystical figure who would appear to Jews in time of trouble, to help the poor, to fight for justice. Since he never really died, many believed him to enjoy a special kind of existence where he could appear or disappear on earth. There are many tales of Eliyahu materializing to right some wrong, often unrecognized—except of course for the teller of the tale and the audience—a kind of superhero for poor Jews, appearing and leaving like the Lone Ranger. This is not a put-down. Poor Jews in trouble needed something—Eliyahu, the Golem—to look to for protection that might not come, but at least they could hope.

He became associated with the seder. The door is opened for him in case he should appear. Some children's tales claim that Eliyahu visits every Jewish house where a seder is being held. Not only is he present or semi-present at every seder, but there is a chair for him at every bris.

We open the door to the outside and sing "Eliyahu Ha-Navi," Eliyahu the Prophet. Eliyahu the Tishbite—his home village. Eliyahu from Gilead—Transjordan, then a wild area. It is as if we were singing Eliyahu from the Yukon. Some people, who have larger dining rooms or fewer guests than we do, leave an empty chair for Eliyahu and set a place for him. I like the symbolism of this, not only for Eliyahu, but for Jews who cannot be present, have no seder to attend, were prevented from carrying out their rituals and practicing their religion freely and openly without danger. But I cannot do this as our dining room is filled completely with the participants, and I regard it as a bigger mitzvah to have as many people as we can handle than to have room for an empty chair.

One reason the door is opened is because of the blood libel.

The first accusation against Jews of murdering Christian children for ritual purposes occurred in Norwich in Britain in 1144 or 1147—different texts give different dates. A boy, William, disappeared on the second day of Passover. A convert said that Jews sacrificed a Christian every year to commemorate the crucifixion. This case seems to have been dismissed, but the story was too attractive to anti-Semites for it to die just because it was invented. The story developed legs and traveled around England, then to the Continent, spreading from France to Germany and finally to Eastern Europe. Blood libel accusations were usually followed by riots, assaults, rape and murder of Jews, confiscation of property, and expulsions from cities or even countries.

Churches and abbeys displayed wonder-working bones of martyrs said to have been slaughtered by Jews during Passover. The usual custom was to arrest and torture Jewish leaders, execute them, and then expel the local community, seizing their property. It was rumored that Jews suffered from strange diseases that could only be cured by the blood, heart, or liver of a male Christian child. As time went on, the accusations became attached to Pesach. Some church leaders announced that these accusations were nonsense, but the blood libel was irresistible to anti-Semites and those who could make a quick profit from the charge. It was popular in thirteenth-century Germany and then took root in Eastern Europe.

The blood libel has persisted through the centuries since, causing mayhem and death, Jews being accused of using Christian blood in the manufacture of matzoh for Pesach. It was used politically in France during the nineteenth century and also in Hungary and in Czarist Russia as late as 1913. The Nazis seized on it in their propaganda.

According to Philip Goodman in *The Passover Anthology* from The Jewish Publication Society, some churches in central and southeastern Europe continue to exhibit pictures and wax statues of Jews in the process of slaughtering a child and collecting his blood. As recently as 1952 a bishop in Austria refused to remove depictions of the blood libel from a church in his jurisdiction, saying that the Jews had never proved they were innocent. This blood libel was a periodic danger to Jews. How many of us died from this story there is no way to know.

Therefore the door was opened wide so that anyone spying on a seder could plainly see that there was no blood in use, nothing to conceal.

In some households, while children are opening the door, the leader of the seder sips some wine from Eliyahu's cup, just enough so that the drop in volume is noticeable. It would be the second act of sleight of hand carried out by the leader.

The spirit of Eliyahu is that of the continuing tradition of prophecy in Judaism, what makes our religion alive and changing. The prophecy of Eliyahu is ongoing in every generation. We are always casting up new Eliyahus with new voices of wisdom and protest and connection. Judaism is alive because it is constantly remade: linked to history, to tradition but also constantly rethought, reimagined, reborn.

The part of the seder we have reached in the traditional haggadah is called the Shefokh Chamatkha, a releasing of anger against those who have oppressed our people and other peoples over the generations. This section was added to the haggadah during the Middle Ages with its periodic massacres of Jews and expulsions. It is therefore a particularly appropriate time to remember the Holocaust and its victims. At some seders, the uprising on Pesach in the Warsaw Ghetto is recalled, as it was on Erev Pesach that the Nazis began the final solution for the Jews of Warsaw and on this evening that those who remained revolted and began armed struggle against an immensely superior force. This is one way we do it at our seder. We say:

Remember: During the Nazi regime, a new and terrible catastrophe entered our history. The story of the Holocaust is our story. We are not free to ignore it or to forget. Therefore, let us remember the women, men and children who faced their end with dignity. Let us remember resistance fighters who fought in the forests or in the Armée Juive Secrète in France, saboteurs, mothers, grandfathers, slave laborers in the factories and the crematoria, those worked to death in the factories at Auschwitz. The famous and the unknown. Artists and peasants. Grandmothers and babies. Those millions who perished and those few who survived. Let us think of them tonight.

Repeat some of the names of the camps and vow never to forget:

AUSCHWITZ-BIRKENAU

MAJDANEK

TREBLINKA

CHELMNO

SOBIBOR

BELZEC

WESTERBORK

BUCHENWALD

MAUTHAUSEN

THERESIENSTADT

BERGEN-BELSEN

RAVENSBRUCK

DORA/NORDHAUSEN

NEUENGAMME

DACHAU

Let us vow never to forget and never to permit this to happen again. As we recite the names of the camps, we again cast drops of wine on our plate.

Some people read a paragraph or two from The Journal of Anne Frank *at this point. Some sing "The Partisan Song."*

We also say, "Let us rejoice that we have reached this night once again to eat unleavened bread and bitter herbs, but let us remember all those who could not celebrate. May we reach other holidays in a time of peace that does not exist now. This toast is to those who have resisted oppression, who have fought back, to those who are resisting, who are fighting back, and to those who will resist, who will fight back."

*A*nother recent addition to the ritual items on the seder table is Miriam's Cup to balance and expand upon Eliyahu's. Miriam is much more strongly associated with Pesach than Eliyahu, since she is one of the major participants in the story. It was Miriam, Moses's older sister, who watched Moses in his little ark in the Nile. When she saw the baby rescued, she offered to find a wet nurse for the baby and brought his mother.

She is referred to as Miriam the Prophet. "And then the prophet Miriam, Aaron's sister, took a timbrel in her hand, and all the women went out after her with timbrels and with dancing" (Exodus 15:20). A timbrel is an instrument struck or shaken in the hand, like a modern tambourine. Miriam led the women in rejoicing on the shore of the Sea of Reeds singing, "Sing to Hashem, for our G-d has triumphed; horse and rider has the Eternal thrown into the sea." This is considered by many scholars to be one of the oldest passages in Torah. Miriam did not sing alone, but with the other women, leading them in a dance and beating the rhythm.

When Miriam was punished for confronting Moses and was shut out of the camp smitten with temporary leprosy for seven days, "the people did not set out on their march until Miriam had been brought into the camp again." In other words, they wouldn't leave without her. Although she was married, Miriam is not noted as somebody's wife or somebody's mother or somebody's daughter—as it true of most of the women the *Tanakh* bothers to name—but she was important and active in her own right. It was Miriam's well that kept the Israelites from dying of thirst in the desert. Therefore, fittingly, her cup contains water. In Midrash it says that when Miriam died, the people were then without water.

I use a clear glass to emphasize the clarity of the water, but many people use a pottery or ceramic cup for her, as for Eliyahu. She is associated with water, often regarded as a female element or symbol: the Nile, the Sea of Reeds, and then her well of clear living water, *mayim chayim*. I remember stories about her from my grandma when I was little: Miriam was strongly associated with Pesach. In Hebrew, *Mar* is the root for bitter and *Yam* means "sea." Miriam's well is also associated with healing. There is an old belief that water drawn from a well on the night just after Shabbat has ended is really from Miriam's well and has healing properties.

Miriam's cup

The cup of Elijah holds wine;
the cup of Miriam holds water.
Wine is more precious
until you have no water.

Water that flows in our veins,
water that is the stuff of life
for we are made of breath
and water, vision

and fact. Elijah is
the extraordinary; Miriam
brings the daily wonders:
the joy of a fresh morning

like a newly prepared table,
a white linen cloth on which
nothing has yet spilled.
The descent into the heavy

waters of sleep healing us.
The scent of bread baking,
roasting chicken, fresh herbs,
the faces of friends across

the table: what sustains us
every morning, every evening,
the common daily miracles
like the taste of cool water.

There are several other women connected with Pesach: the midwives Shifra and Puah, who saved as many male Hebrew babies as they were able, in spite of the Pharaoh's edict that they were to be killed; Yocheved, the mother of Moses, who hid him as long as she could, for three months, then made a little ark sealed watertight with pitch in order to preserve his life; even the Egyptian princess without a name who decided to raise Moses in spite of guessing that he was a Hebrew baby, thus defying her father and revealing her own compassion that leapt boundaries and found the offspring of slaves worth her care. As the traditional haggadah says, quoting the Babylonian Talmud, it is because of the righteousness of the women of that generation that we were redeemed from Egypt. Shifra and Puah were slaves, yet they dared to defy the violent order from Pharaoh, the most powerful man in Egypt, who was treated as a god. They revolted and said that the Hebrew women delivered the babies before they could arrive.

In Micah 6:4, the Eternal is depicted as saying, "For I brought you up from the land of Egypt and from the house of slavery; and I sent you Moses, Aaron, and Miriam." It is about time that we placed a cup for Miriam on the seder table, for she has a far more real connection with Pesach than anyone we mention except Moses. Debbie Friedman has written a song about Miriam for Pesach, which you might locate and learn and perhaps sing together. The great feminist poet Muriel Rukeyser also has a poem about Miriam.

If at Pesach we think about our personal Mitzrayim, our own tight place of bondage, whether to inner or outer forces, then when remembering Miriam we should particularly consider how women have been bound, sometimes actually, sometimes by words or customs, sometimes by law, sometimes by what we have been taught to call love or loyalty to husband, boyfriend, or family. Our feet have been bound, our wombs have been claimed, our bodies mutilated by clitoridectomy, by all the tortures of a search for plastic beauty—silicon breasts, liposuction, face-lifts, tummy tucks, all the ways the society encourages us to "improve" our- selves while neglecting our minds, our characters, true and useful knowledge. Women have been rendered *agunah*, neither with nor without a husband but stuck in a middle place of bondage to a custom that demeans them. Women are in bondage when they have no control over their own bodies. If my body is not mine, then I am a slave. If I am not to be only half a human being, then I must join with others to fight to be whole. Only a slave has no control over her own body, no choice. To be free means to be free to choose what to do, where to live, how to live, when to bear and when not to bear children. It is to be free to discover our own seasons of our bodies, our lives, our times, and align ourselves with what we find true and righteous.

Miriam is an important figure to remember during the seder not only because she was directly involved with our liberation from slavery and in the creation of the Jewish people as a nation but also because she was a strong woman, an uppity woman, one who faced the consequences of standing up for herself and who took care of her people to the best of her ability, which was not negligible. She watched over Moses when he was a helpless baby; she made sure he was raised by his own mother; she was obvi- ously a leader, especially of the women, and she saved her people in the desert by finding water, not once but many times. Water is simple, water is bland, water just is, we think, until we are without it. There is no life for us without water. We are largely composed of water. Miriam's element is close to life itself. Therefore on Pesach now we celebrate her, as women have often done over the millennia.

You can create a toast or blessing over the cup of clear precious water, one that reflects women's strength or what women have endured and do endure, or a toast that looks to the future equality and safety for women. You might say over the cup a rededication to women's freedom and safety.

Miriam's well is a powerful symbol of clarity, of truth-seeking, of inspiration. The Safed mystics, who created the notion of Shabbat as a bride, believed in Miriam's well as a source of inspiration. Legends say that they found it anew and that it cleared their minds and hearts and enabled them to understand Torah far more clearly. Sometimes Miriam's well stands for the collective understanding, creativity, and knowledge of women in Judaism. The presence of Miriam's cup on the seder table beside that devoted to Eliyahu reminds us of the importance of women in the Exodus, that one of the three leaders was a woman, that women were intimately and actively involved—something that has dropped out of sight during patriarchal seders and the traditional haggadah. It also reminds us how much women have to contribute to Judaism, when we are let in the door and encouraged to speak up, or when we simply demand a role.

Some people who use Miriam's cup in their seders do so by talking about her during the Maggid section of the haggadah. Others, like me, talk about her in connection with Eliyahu's cup, in the section of the haggadah after the meal. Either way, surely she belongs in our seders, now more than ever. It is only since the late '70s that we have consciously put her back in the Exodus story, but she never really left it. I remember a song from my grandma's seder about Miriam dancing in some wonderful future time when Massiach had come. I think Jewish women have always remembered her and have seen her as one of our special foremothers.

After we raise Miriam's cup we should say a blessing. You may well want to make up your own.

This water we bless and drink in honor of all the women who stayed in the kitchen cooking and serving and never got to sit down and join in the seder. This water we bless for all the women who told their daughters and granddaughters stories that made Jewish life and history meaningful and vivid to them. This water we bless for all the women who invented the various traditions of food we cherish and enjoy today, passed on from kitchen to kitchen, from woman to woman. This water we bless for all the women who were kept from the learning they craved, who could not learn and teach, who could not sing in shul, who could not preach what they burned to say, who could not lead services. This water we bless for all the women who are working now to renew Judaism and pass on a more giving, a more equal, a more woman-oriented Judaism.

Then we take a sip of water, for that is what sustains our lives.

22
Songs and Ending

𝕬fter the intense third section, the last part is mostly singing. You have a wide choice. Whatever haggadah you are using probably has lyrics, preferably with music. Some songs are traditional. But you can select any you like and that enough people know. I have tried incorporating beautiful songs I have found while researching Pesach, but unless I send the music to some participants beforehand and ask them to practice the songs, and they actually do, the unfamiliar falls flat and nobody chimes in.

Psalms 115 through 118, followed by Psalm 136, are traditional. Other traditional songs are "Echad Mi Yode'a," which I actually learned in Yiddish at my grandmother's seders as "Mu Asapru"; "Adir Hu," which we always sing; and "Chad Gadya." In my childhood I took a dislike to that song which has never really vanished. I thought it was mean and I worried about all the creatures. During the seder, we have sung "Mah Nishtana," "Zum Gali Gali," "Dayenu," "Lo Yisa Goy," a Birkat Ha-Mazon, "Hine Mah Tov," and "Eliyahu Ha-Navi." In the last section, we also sing a Yiddish song:

Shabbas, Shabbas,
Zoll zein, zoll zein Shabbas
Shabbas, Shabbas
Zoll zein, zoll zein, zoll zein, zoll zein Shabbas.

Yubba bubba, bubba bubba bim bim bim   (*repeated*)

Pesach, Pesach
Zoll zein, zoll zein Pesach, etc.

Shalom, shalom, etc.

In other words, let there continue to be whatever you are cherishing in the song. Then we go around the table and whoever wants to, adds something, usually in English, like "friends" or "children" or "chocolate" or whatever they feel like celebrating, that they wish to continue to exist. It can be serious or silly, as above.

We've done the partisan song in the segment that deals with the Holocaust. In the last section, we sometimes sing "Oseh Shalom." We finish the seder with the following poems; the second one we always do and the first one we have been reading in wartime:

Peace in a time of war

A puddle of amber light
like sun spread on a table,

food flirting savor into the nose
faces of friends, a vase
of daffodils and Dutch iris:

this is an evening of honey
on the tongue, cinnamon
scented, red wine sweet
and dry, voices rising
like a flock of swallows

turning together in evening
air. Darkness walls off
the room from what lies
outside, the fire and dust
and blood of war, bodies

stacked like firewood,
burst like overripe melons.
Ceremony is a moat we have
crossed into a moment's
harmony, as if the world paused—

but it doesn't. What we must
do waits like coats tossed
on the bed, that we'll rise
from this warm table
put on again and go out.

*Let us drink the fourth cup of wine to a hopeful future, toasting those who
work to make the world better, more peaceful and with more justice for
everyone. Let us pledge ourselves to be among those who try to do just that.*

*Barukha Yah Shekinah
Eloheinu malkat ha-olom
borey pri ha-gafen.*

Often people like to read something particularly meaningful to
them at this point, something that sums up in some way what has
come before or something that is a call toward what each must
hope to do in the coming year, the resolves renewed, the tasks
uncompleted but awaiting our attention. We use this poem:

The art of blessing the day

*This is the blessing for rain after drought:
Come down, wash the air so it shimmers,
a perfumed shawl of lavender chiffon.
Let the parched leaves suckle and swell.
Enter my skin, wash me for the little
chrysalis of sleep rocked in your plashing.
In the morning the world is peeled to shining.*

*This is the blessing for sun after long rain:
Now everything shakes itself free and rises.
The trees are bright as pushcart ices.
Every last lily opens its satin thighs.
The bees dance and roll in pollen*

and the cardinal at the top of the pine
sings at full throttle, fountaining.

This is the blessing for a ripe peach:
This is luck made round. Frost can nip
the blossom, kill the bee. It can drop,
a hard green useless nut. Brown fungus,
the burrowing worm that coils in rot can
blemish it and wind crush it on the ground.
Yet this peach fills my mouth with juicy sun.

This is the blessing for the first garden tomato:
Those green boxes of tasteless acid the store
sells in January, those red things with the savor
of wet chalk, they mock your fragrant name.
How fat and sweet you are weighing down my palm,
warm as the flank of a cow in the sun.
You are the savor of summer in a thin red skin.

This is the blessing for a political victory:
Although I shall not forget that things
work in increments and epicycles and sometime
leaps that half the time fall back down,
let's not relinquish dancing while the music
fits into our hips and bounces our heels.
We must never forget, pleasure is real as pain.

The blessing for the return of a favorite cat,
the blessing for love returned, for friends'

return, for money received unexpected,
the blessing for the rising of the bread,
the sun, the oppressed. I am not sentimental
about old men mumbling the Hebrew by rote
with no more feeling than one says gesundheit.

But the discipline of blessings is to taste
each moment, the bitter, the sour, the sweet
and the salty, and be glad for what does not
hurt. The art is in compressing attention
to each little and big blossom of the tree
of life, to let the tongue sing each fruit,
its savor, its aroma and its use.

Attention is love, what we must give
children, mothers, fathers, pets,
our friends, the news, the woes of others.
What we want to change we curse and then
pick up a tool. Bless whatever you can
with eyes and hands and tongue. If you
can't bless it, get ready to make it new.

We then say something like this:

We have once again celebrated and recited the ancient epic of Israel's
liberation from bondage and learned the message of Exodus. We have
rededicated ourselves to the cause of freedom and repair of the world. As we
have celebrated this festival tonight, so may we celebrate it, all of us
together, next year again, in joy, in freedom, and in peace. Now we are

here. Next year, may we be in the City of Jerusalem. Now we dream of freedom. We dream of a world at peace. May the coming year bring freedom to the oppressed, peace to Zion and Jerusalem and the world.

We finish with "Shalom Chaverim."

Shalom chaverim, shalom chaverim, shalom, shalom, l'hitra'ot, l'hitra'ot, shalom, shalom.

Shalom chaverim, shalom chaverim, shalom, shalom l'kol ha-olam, l'kol ha-olam, shalom, shalom.

(Peace, friends, peace, friends, peace, see you again soon. Peace, friends, peace, friends, peace, peace to all the world, peace.)

Go in peace into the springtime and be renewed.

The important thing here is to have a sense of closure but one that should lead people forward into their daily lives with new intent and resolve. They should understand that their year's journey has only begun.

At some seders, they include a number of spirituals, such as "Go Tell It on the Mountain," "Let My People Go," "Down by the Riverside," "We Shall Overcome," "This Little Light of Mine," and whatever you may like. Almost anything joyful and energetic you feel like singing and that others in the group know or can follow works just fine. Some do a few Beatles songs.

As we complete our seders, let us remember about Judaism that it is made by each of us new and again and constantly. As the kabbalah teaches us in the *Zohar*, when the revelation came at Sinai, every Jew yet to be born was present also, and each heard a different piece of the truth. The Oral Torah is never finished because we all have pieces of wisdom to add. Judaism is alive today because it has been continually remade and renewed. Let us each give our piece of the truth to one another and the future before we die. So let us come to every seder of every year expecting not just a meal and to see family and friends, but to reconnect to our history, our traditions, our *mitzvot*, our duty to repair the world.

It is traditional to finish the seder with *"l'shanah ha-ba'ah b'Yerushalayim"*—"Next year in Jerusalem." In the bad times that have come so frequently during the Diaspora, this made sense as a wish for escape, for a homeland, for some place that was Jewish and free instead of a ghetto or the Pale. During the Holocaust, it had great poignancy. Now that there is Israel, usually embattled, some Jews say it as fervently as ever, and some balk at the phrase.

But Jerusalem the golden, the city on a hill, is actually two. One is physical, divided and fought over for millennia. The other is the city of peace we have never attained. Utopias come in two forms: the garden—the pastoral utopia—and the city of peace. Although the Torah begins with a garden, we have been mostly city dwellers long enough to find an image of the ideal city, the city of equality and peace and justice, one of our strongest images of the Good Place on earth. Everyone, regardless of their opinions of the government or actions of Israel, whether for, against, neutral, or confused, can wish to be next year in a city of peace and plenty, of equality and freedom for all who dwell in it. Even if we never arrive, as Moses didn't, we can still strive toward that city, continuing our journey and our work together.

The end of the seder invites us each to think about the coming year and what we hope to accomplish, what we choose to work for or against, how we decide to use our energies and our resources.

Every year after the seder is completed and the songs are sung, we sit around the table and tell jokes. Some of them are specifically Jewish jokes; some are not. The kids always have jokes they like to tell, and they love to hear the grown-ups tell off-color jokes. It lightens everything after an intense evening. We finish catching up, but the bulk of that was done before the seder started and during the meal. Mostly it's a relaxed, almost silly time. The kids go off to find the cats, who have been shut up during the seder (gefilte fish, chicken soup, and gedempte flaisch are just too tempting). The table is cleared by whoever wants to help. The first load goes in the dishwasher. Many of the participants will not see each other until the following Pesach, when they will have more stories to tell; jobs begun, well done, or lost; babies born; spouses changed or acquired. Another annual cycle has come to its fruition and its completion. Next year if not in Jerusalem, then in my dining room. May your seder be as fulfilling as the food is filling! May you go into the springtime night with your mind as engaged as your digestive system. May you carry away from your seder a sense of renewal and rededication. Mazel tov.

Bibliography

Some Passover Books I Found Useful:

Anisfeld, Sharon Cohen, Tara Mohr, and Catherine Spector. *The Women's Passover Companion: Women's Reflections on the Festival of Freedom.* Woodstock, Vt.: Jewish Lights, 2003.

————. *The Woman's Seder Sourcebook: Rituals and Readings for Use at the Passover Seder.* Woodstock, Vt.: Jewish Lights, 2003.

Arnow, David. *Creating Lively Passover Seders: A Sourcebook of Engaging Tales, Texts & Activities.* Woodstock, Vt.: Jewish Lights, 2004.

Bergant, Dianne. "An anthropological approach to biblical interpretation." *Semeia* 67 (1994): pp. 43–62.

Bynum, Caroline Walker. *Holy Feast and Holy Fast.* Berkeley: University of California Press, 1987.

Dundes, Alan, ed. *The Blood Libel Legend: A Casebook in Anti-Semitic Folklore.* Norman, Okla.: University of Oklahoma Press, 1971.

Ehrlich, Elizabeth. *Miriam's Kitchen: A Memoir.* New York: Penguin Books, 1997.

Fredman, Ruth Gruber. *The Passover Seder: Afikoman in Exile.* Philadelphia: University of Pennsylvania Press, 1981.

Goodman, Philip. *The Passover Anthology.* Philadelphia: Jewish Publication Society, 1961.

Greenberg, Irving. *The Jewish Way: Living the Holidays.* New York: Touchstone Books, 1993.

Kimmel, Eric A. *Wonders and Miracles: A Passover Companion.* New York: Scholastic Press, 2004.

Laufer, Nathan. *Leading the Passover Journey: The Seder's Meaning Revealed.* Woodstock, Vt.: Jewish Lights, 2005.

Marx, Alexander. *Studies in Jewish History and Booklore.* New York: The Jewish Theological Society of America, 1944.

Strassfeld, Michael. *Holidays: A Guide and Commentary.* Philadelphia: Jewish Publication Society, 1985.

Waskow, Arthur I. *Seasons of Our Joy: A Handbook of Jewish Festivals.* New York: Summit Books, 1982.

Wolfson, Ron. *Passover: The Family Guide to Spiritual Celebration, The Art of Jewish Living,* 2nd ed.,Woodstock, Vt.: Jewish Lights Publishing, 2002.

Zerner, Moshe. *Evolving Halakhah: A Progressive Approach to Traditional Jewish Law.* Woodstock, Vt.: Jewish Lights, 1999.

Haggadahs

Ben-Khayyim, Dov, ed. *The Telling: A Loving Haggadah for Passover.* Berkeley, Calif.:, Rakhamim Publications, 1989.

Cohen, Steven F., and Kenneth Brander. *The Yeshiva University Haggadah.* New York: Student Organization of Yeshiva, 1985.

Glazer, Nathan, ed. *The Schocken Passover Haggadah.* New York: Schocken Books, 1981.

Kaplan, Mordecai M., Eugene Kohn, and Ira Eisenstein, eds. *The New Haggadah,* rev. ed. New York: Jewish Reconstructionist Foundation/Behrman House, 1978.

Levitt, Joy, and Michael Strassfeld, eds. *A Night of Questions: A Passover Haggadah*. Elkins Park, Penn.: The Reconstructionist Press, 2000.

Levy, Richard N. *On Wings of Freedom: The Hillel Haggadah for the Nights of Passover*. Hoboken, N.J.: B'nai B'rith Hillel Foundation in association with Ktav, 1989.

Schuldenfrei, Jack, and Joel Harris. *The 4th World Haggadah*. London: World Union of Jewish Students, 1970.

Sheinson, Yosef Dov. *A Survivors' Haggadah*, edited with an introduction and commentary by Saul Touster. Philadelphia: Jewish Publication Society, 2000.

Sholom Aleichem Club of Philadelphia. *Haggadah for a Secular Celebration of Pesach*. Philadelphia, undated.

Zones, J. *San Diego Women's Haggadah*, 2nd ed., San Diego: Woman's Institute for Continuing Jewish Education, 1986.

Food

Allen, Stewart Lee. *In the Devil's Garden: A Sinful History of Forbidden Food*. New York: Ballantine Books, 2002.

Avrutick, Frances R. *The Complete Passover Cookbook*. New York: Jonathan David, 1987.

Brown, Michael. *The Jewish Gardening Cookbook*. Woodstock, Vt.: Jewish Lights, 1998.

Cooper, John. *Eat and Be Satisifed: A Social History of Jewish Food*. Northvale, N.J.: Jason Aronson, 1993.

Couniham, Carole M. *The Anthropology of Food and Body: Gender, Meaning and Power*. New York: Routledge, 1999.

Douglas, Mary. *Purity and Danger: An Analysis of Concepts of Pollution and Taboo*. London: Routledge, 1966.

Eidlitz, E. *Is It Kosher: An Encyclopedia of Kosher Foods, Facts, and Fallacies*. Jerusalem: Feldheim, 1992.

Elkort, Martin. *The Secret Life of Food: A Feast of Food and Drink History, Folklore, and Fact.* Los Angeles: J.P. Tarcher, 1991.

Fernandes-Armesto, Felipe. *Near a Thousand Tables: A History of Food.* New York: Free Press, 2002.

Frank, Nicole Barchilon. *Divine Delights: Persian, French, and Sephardic Savors from the Kitchen of Nicole Barchilon Frank.* Unpublished, 2004.

Harris, Marvin. *Good to Eat: Riddles of Culture and Food.* New York: Simon & Schuster, 1985.

Kiple, Kenneth F., ed. *The Cambridge World History of Food.* New York: Cambridge University Press, 2003.

Kurlansky, Mark. *Salt: A World History.* New York: Walker, 2002.

McGovern, Patrick E. *Ancient Wine: The Search for the Origins of Viniculture.* Princeton, N.J.: Princetown University Press, 2003.

McPhee, John. *The Founding Fish.* New York: Farrar, Straus, and Giroux, 2002.

Nabhan, Gary Paul. *Some Like It Hot: Food, Genes and Cultural Diversity.* Washington, D.C.: Island Press, 2004.

Percy, Pam. *The Complete Chicken: An Entertaining History of Chickens.* New York: Random House, 1978.

Pollan, Michael. *The Botany of Desire: A Plant's Eye View of the World.* New York: Random House, 2001.

Rousso, Nira. *The Passover Gourmet.* New York: Adama Books, 1987.

Schwartz, Oded. *In Search of Plenty: A History of Jewish Food.* London: Kyle Cathie, 1992.

Tannahill, Reay. *Food in History.* New York: Crown, 1989.

Whitman, Sylvia. *What's Cooking: The History of American Food.* Minneapolis, Minn.: Lerner Publications, 2001.

Wright, Clifford. *A Mediterranean Feast.* New York: William Morrow, 1999.

Poem Titles

Poem acknowledgments

From The Art of Blessing the Day
   (*New York: Alfred A. Knopf,* 2000):
"The art of blessing the day"
"Beitzeh"
"Charoset"
"Chazeret"
"Karpas"
"Lamb Shank—Z'roah Pesach"
"Learning to read"
"Maggid"
"Maror"
"Matzoh"
"The task never completed"
"The wine"
"Salt water"

From Colors Passing Through Us
   (New York: Alfred A. Knopf, 2003):
"Miriam's cup"
"Tapuz: an orange"

From Circles on the Water
   (New York: Alfred A. Knopf, 1982):
"The love of lettuce"

"The cup of Eliyahu," *Midstream*, vol. XXXXIX, No. 3, April 2003.
"Peace in a time of war," *Tikkun*, Vol. 19, No. 5, September/October, 2004.
These two poems are contained in *The Crooked Inheritance*, Knopf, October
   2006.

Recipes

Meat and Poultry Dishes

Desserts

A Note on the Type

The text of this book was set in Weiss, a typeface designed in
Germany by Emil Rudolf Weiss (1875–1942). The design of
the roman was completed in 1928 and that of the italic in
1931. Both are well balanced and even in color, and both
reflect the subtle skill of a fine calligrapher.

COMPOSED BY
Creative Graphics, Allentown, Pennsylvania

PRINTED AND BOUND BY
RR Donnelley, Harrisonburg, Virginia

DESIGNED BY
Iris Weinstein

LIBRARY DISCARD